METAPHYSICAL DIVINE WISDOM

on Universal, Physical, Spiritual and Soul Love

A Practical Motivational Guide to Spirituality Series

KEVIN HUNTER

WARRIOR OF LIGHT PRESS

The author of this book does not dispense medical advice or prescribe the use of any technique as a form of treatment for physical, emotional, or medical problems without the advice of a physician, either directly or indirectly. The intent of the author is only to offer information of a general nature to help you in your quest for emotional and spiritual well-being. In the event, you use any of the information in this book for yourself, which is your constitutional right, the author and the publisher assume no responsibility for your actions.

Warrior of Light Press
www.kevin-hunter.com

First Edition: July 2019
Printed in the United States of America

ISBN-13: 978-1-7331962-5-3

3. Mind and Body. 2. Spirituality. 1. Title

DEDICATION

For you on your soul's spiritual journey.

METAPHYSICAL DIVINE WISDOM
BOOK SERIES

On Psychic Spirit Team Heaven Communication
On Soul Consciousness and Purpose
On Increasing Prayer with Faith for an Abundant Life
On Balancing the Mind, Body, and Soul
On Manifesting Fearless Assertive Confidence
On Universal, Physical, Spiritual and Soul Love

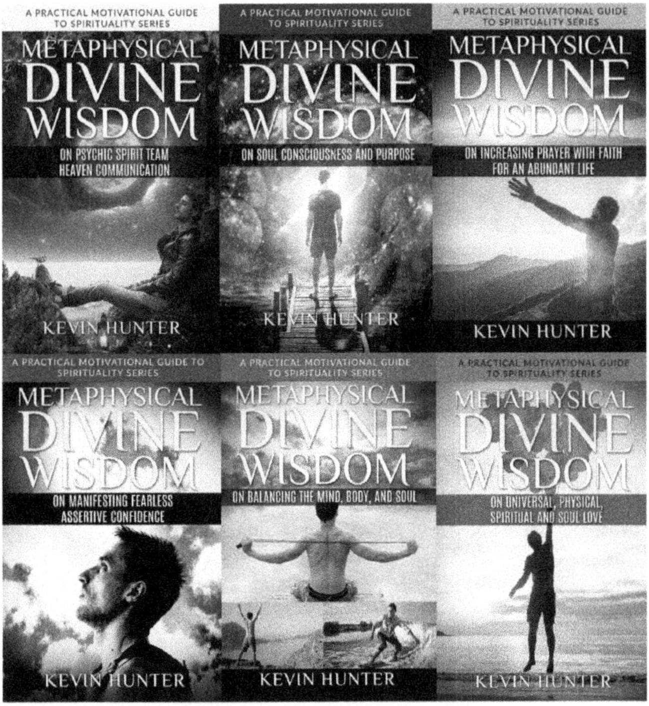

♥

Contents

AUTHOR NOTE

The *Metaphysical Divine Wisdom* books are a series of spiritually based books that focus on different areas of one's life. Like many of my spiritual related metaphysical books, this one is also infused with practical messages and spirit guidance that my Spirit team has taught and shared with me revolving around many different topics. The main goal is to fine-tune your body, mind, and soul. Like all souls, you are a Divine communicator capable of receiving messages and guidance from Heaven.

My personal Spirit team council makes up God and the Holy Spirit, as well as a team of guides, angels, and sometimes Archangels and Saints. I am merely the liaison or messenger in delivering and interpreting the intentions of what they wish to communicate. My team comprises some hard truth telling Wise Ones from the Other Side, including Saint Nathaniel, who can be brutal in his direct forcefulness. He cuts right to the heart of humanity without apology. I have learned quite a bit from him while adopting his ideology, which is Heaven's philosophy as a whole. I wouldn't preach Divine Guidance that God doesn't whisper into my Clairaudient ear first.

If I use the word "He" when pertaining to God, this does not mean that I am advocating that he is a male. Simply replace the word, "He" with one you are comfortable using to identify God for you to be. If the word, "God" makes you uncomfortable, then substitute it with one you're more familiar with like Universe, Spirit, the Light, or any other comparable word. This goes for any gender I use as examples. When I say, "spirit team", I am referring to a team of 'Guides and Angels'.

One of the purposes of my work is to empower, enlighten, as well as entertain. It's also to help you improve yourself, your soul, your life and humanity by default. If anything, I am preaching to myself, because God knows that I can use a refresher course once in a while. It does not matter if you are a beginner or well versed in the subject matter. There may be something that reminds you of something you already know or something that you were unaware of. We all have much to share with one another, as we are all one in the end.

~ Kevin Hunter

METAPHYSICAL DIVINE WISDOM

ON UNIVERSAL, PHYSICAL, SPIRITUAL AND SOUL LOVE

CHAPTER ONE

It's All About Love

The point of all existence in the end is connected to love, whether that is love for another person, self-love, or universal and spiritual love. One of the main reasons all souls are here is to learn the nature of love. Perhaps you're incredible at running a business, accumulating money, and helping people physically survive by keeping them employed. This is one of your life purposes, but when you pass on you will not be taking any of that with you. If you haven't learned anything about love, then what was the point?

In one of the episodes of James Lipton's *Inside the Actor's Studio*, he interviews actress Sharon

Stone. She tells him a story about a friend of hers that was dying of AIDS. She explained that she would visit him regularly in the Hospital. There was a point when he was cutting in and out of death. When he cut back into this reality his whole expression changed. He said, "Oh my god, oh my god!"

Sharon was filled with emotion, "What? What is it? Tell me?"

He said, "It's all about love."

Sharon grabbed her chest choking back tears head slumped down with emotion.

It's all about love.

Some souls choose to incarnate into an Earthly life in order to experience all of the Earthly physical pleasures from sex, food, and music, making love, falling in love, loving love to spreading love. Love is an in-depth complicated word with various meanings beyond being in a love relationship. Love is difficult to pin down since the meaning is much deeper than the surface. It can be an intense satisfying appreciation or approving supportive expression for someone or something. Love can be putting passion and heart into whatever you do in life. It's making choices from the heart, rather than rationalizing it through the mind, which can talk you out of doing something you are more than capable of.

Love is to understand that even the most heinous person in your eyes has love built into them deep down in the core of their soul. When you are in Heaven you truly understand what Universal love is like. While on Earth there is no such thing as Universal love when it comes to human beings thanks to the domination of the Darkness that controls the human ego. Human beings are the one species incapable of displaying Universal love. Some may claim to love everybody, but when you dive into the governing human ego, then it's easy to detect that this is just not true. There are exceptions moving about on this planet. They are the rare people that see the good in all they come across no matter what. We call those spirits Incarnated Angels living in a human body, because their compassionate personalities are like that of an angel. Angels are egoless and see the love within all souls including the most heinous human being on the planet. This doesn't mean they're approving of that person enacting violence or hatred, but they have this keen psychic ability to see beneath the surface. They know who that soul was at its conception, which was 100% love.

It's an impossible request to demand that someone with an ego that is constantly susceptible to being captured by the Darkness display Universal love. It's almost an unreasonable request to place on a human being to show love for someone that caused harm on another person. One Mother was somehow able to do that with her son's killer demanding that instead of condemning him to punishment that he be treated for his "sickness". Many applauded that Mother for being able to do something that almost no one can do.

It is not unreasonable to request that someone show love to those you don't understand. Skim all of the attacks on social media accounts like Twitter and you'll find that 99% of them are misplaced and unnecessary. It's all bathed in dark ego, anger, stress, and lower distracting energies that change no hearts or minds. Sadly, it is also what is popular on social media. The dark ego is fed through drama achieving a drug like high off it. This is what fills social media accounts to the brim of some kind of non-constructive rant about someone or something they despise. This isn't about the occasional slip that an overall positive person falls into where they suddenly take a moment to complain about something. This is about the regular offenders where the majority of their posts are negatively based every hour of every day. It doesn't do anything to help matters. It certainly doesn't contribute to bringing more love into the world. Someone looking to bring more love into the world already knows this won't help their causes.

You may find someone to be monstrous, while another person has a deeper understanding of that person. Someone tells me about someone that enacted a horrible crime. Others will immediately jump into the hang him rhetoric, but I want to understand what propelled the person to do something. I've forever been fascinated with the complexities of the nature of human beings and all of the details that it encompasses. This includes wanting to understand what makes someone on Earth the way they are, because they certainly weren't born that way.

While human beings are flawed and will inevitably mess up when their ego rules the roost, it is spirits love that is constant and unwavering.

When I connect with God and Spirit, they pull me up into a wave of love that is better than anything I've ever experienced, and I've experienced plenty! I couldn't write thousands of pages of text without them, especially with my restless ADD *(attention deficit disorder).* We found that the one area my ADD is not present is when I'm writing, which is no doubt a sign of Divine intervention and guidance.

If one is too absorbed on the surface of things to comprehend what's going on beyond the physical, then it is unlikely they are in touch with the psychic touch. The touch is being in tune to spirit and the vibrations from beyond. It doesn't mean they are incapable of that kind of deep spirit connection, because they do have the power deep down within them to access it. Every single soul has that same power, whether they know it or not, and regardless of their human belief limitations.

It would be awesome if every single person on the planet was keenly aware of their innate psychic abilities built into their soul's DNA, because then Earth would be as close to Heaven as feasibly possible. There would be never-ending joy, peace, and love for every soul. Everyone would be operating from a higher vibration while moving mountains in the process. We see this kind of amazing uplifting joy in others when they're in a high vibrational state. Because this is not the current reality where everyone is functioning in that space, this makes Earthly life more challenging than it should be. It is either us or other people that create the majority of problems that happen in the physical world. Once in a while, Mother Earth creates catastrophes, since this rock we temporarily inhabit has a life force of its own. If you want to see a horrific allegory symbolism that proves it's point as to how Mother Earth is a living breathing organism, then watch a film like *Mother!* with Jennifer Lawrence. It was a film that was both supremely loved and venomously hated. You know a piece of art did its job when it creates such opposing reactions in people.

The dead are amongst us on Earth, but they're not dead in the way one might believe them to be dead. They're no longer weighed down and strangled by this ego dominated false reality that force-feeds a fictional superficial shallow view of human life. The real death and Hell is living on a planet that lacks in love with minimal to no awareness or mind-blowing perception. This isn't saying that no one is like that because there are a great many souls on the planet that are filled with love, operate from love, and give love. They also have enormous awareness and mind-blowing foresight. The majority on the planet does not reside in that space. Because if they did, then that would be evident in the physical world's culture and it's not. The dominant rule on Earth is the darkness of ego. This is why one quarter of the planet is here with a purpose to counter that with their Light. You are a way shower in this manner even if it changes one person that ends up changing another and so forth. This is how a mighty positive love movement of change happens Universally.

We have been moving into a period where

more souls are incarnating with this grand awareness of love. There has been a growing movement of people seeking ways to find fulfillment and happiness. Some call this the New Age, but it's not New Age but the soul's reality. If the New Age is about displaying love, then feel free to drink a healthy helping of it. The New Age teaches about self-love and that you are your own authority. To one extent this is true, but there is a higher authority that some call God, the Universe, Spirit, or however you choose to label it. Many will fidget or grow uncomfortable when the word God is said. This is due to the excessive negative way it's been used in horrific ways by Nazi-like fanatical religious groups. They will hide behind the God or Jesus Christ name to harm, hate, and harass other people claiming they're doing it out of love. Regardless of what label you choose to use, God is the ultimate authority to partner with in order to find that eternal love within that brings true soul happiness. Human beings cannot do everything alone and why would you want to when you have willing spirit guardians around you on call and available to help, protect, and guide you to become a stronger person and a more evolved soul in the process.

Being all love and light is a great quality to have, but you also cannot be naïve to other elements that are alive and affecting a great many souls around the planet. There may be quite a bit of the love and light stuff being pushed into the ethers. Being happy and filled with joy and positivity is a wonderful state to achieve, but ignoring everything else as if it doesn't exist can cause problems too. You cannot fully understand the Light if you don't have an understanding of the Dark. Life is not all cute stuffed animals, flowers, and cuddles.

The Light souls on Earth do their best to stay away from anyone that resides in a lower energy space. They can detect when to steer clear of the dark energies due to having a vastly tuned-in calibrated psychic antennae. They move towards those that reside in a higher vibrational Light state, while the darker human soul attracts in others that reside in a negative space. Their negative energy grows more repressed as the Dark energies take over, while the stronger sensitive soul rises like helium above the Darkness and into the vortex of the Light where love resides.

A person's Guardian Angel and Spirit Guide are always near the person they're assigned to in many ways on varying levels. Being connected to them is like having a best friend in another dimension. Like God, these are beings that know everything about you including all of the good and the bad. They know your thoughts and feelings, the things you hide, the things you reveal, and yet they never leave your side. They continue to love you unconditionally no matter how horrific a human crime you've done, which isn't saying that you won't need to pay for that crime depending on the severity.

One of their jobs is to support and guide you on the right path. This includes through paying for karma created. When you act out and cause trouble in school, then you're sent to the principal's office to be disciplined. The soul class works in a similar way, but some of the soul crimes are not all the same as the Earthly crimes. If you're headed towards danger, then they do their best to stop you or steer you away from that. This is why it's important to be clear minded and to develop a strong connection with them. It helps you decipher between a good decision and a bad one when you're tuned in to them daily.

I was never trained to call on the Angels, Archangels, or Guides, nor do I practice yoga or meditate, not that I have any problem with anyone that does, because I have many friends in the spiritual communities that do. We all respect our own ways of doing things with love and without judgment. As a restless driven warrior soldier, my soul's physical energy charges forward with more energy than those decades younger than I. It's always been like that and hasn't stopped yet, but this restless fighter soul energy from back home in Heaven is infused into the human part of me. This makes it challenging for me to sit still and meditate or do yoga exercises, because it's not how my soul was made. When I'm in nature I may sit or lie down to kick back and absorb God's uplifting healing love energy for a bit, then I'll stroll on foot to breathe it all in. This is how I personally connect with Spirit to have their love envelop me, but what works for me may not work for you.

I grew up in a volatile abusive home that was lacking in love. Something like that would break most people. When it broke me, it would only do so for a minute or two, but then I'd be lifted back up. God and my Spirit team would reappear refusing to allow me to be broken down by any of the poor human circumstances I was stuck in at the time. God loved and strengthened me back to life and into complete spiritual centeredness. Every day when I wake up from sleep it feels like a new dawn where I'm renewed with feel good feelings of love again. This is regardless of what my state was in the day before. If it was a bad day the day before, then I pray, go to bed, I wake up fully healed and restored with an optimistic attitude ready and revved to go again. One of the first thoughts to my Spirit team is, "What do you want me to accomplish today?" To this day, I still converse with God and my Spirit team each morning.

Having been raised in a violent abusive household with parents that struggled with money adds to the differing perception of human life than those growing up in a less dysfunctional environment. Growing up not loved by any human being gave me an enlightening lesson. I didn't need to be loved by anyone, because the love I was getting from above was stronger, loyal, long lasting, and more powerful than any human being is capable of giving. This empowered me to rise up in warrior mode. If I have to go it alone, I'll go it alone, I've done it before and succeeded.

Every soul is made by God, which is why some see Him as their parent, rather than their own parents. Souls reside in different areas, realms, and dimensions in Heaven. Some call it the spirit world when there are more spirit worlds than just one.

Spirits are not all in the same place as they are on Earth. Even though all souls can travel wherever they choose to be. They still like to have one place they call home even on the Other Side, just like on Earth. If a soul is a free-spirited soul in Heaven, they may have a place they call their home base, even if they're out and about traveling through all of the infinite vast spaces that exist in Heaven. Souls look to see where they can be of use, since all souls love to be of service in some way. On Earth, you may be trained to serve yourself, but in Heaven we serve others under the Light.

Some people will continue to repeat another human life the way you go to another grade in School to continue your education. This is with the hopes that the soul will have that breakthrough into their consciousness that prompts them to evolve out of the limited consciousness they were previously residing in. Regardless of which part you reside in Heaven, all souls are free, courageous, and fearless. They all display joy, love, peace and high-octane upbeat energy always. It's what truly being alive feels like if one could get that way naturally without any toxins or substances.

When it came to my spiritual work, I was more interested in helping people learn to make sounder choices in life, love more often, live more peacefully, joyfully, and obtain their goals. I knew that if they were connecting to a higher power themselves that it could positively help them reach those things, while also knowing there was more to life than the physical mundane trained early on.

Earthly life is tough for more people than not,

but it is especially tough on the sensitive souls. It is the ultra-sensitive that psychically see, feel, know, and hear more than the average soul. It can be challenging to stay centered in a world that doesn't believe in that, understand it, or care for that matter. This is a clue that you came here for a reason, even if that reason is to shine that bright light of love that is your basic nature to all you encounter.

The highest vibrational energy that exists is love. This isn't to be confused with the kind of love bond two people have, but this is more of a universal love. To understand love is to be able to peer into the heart of a human being. The heart part of you is your soul. It is who you truly are behind the physical and personality part of yourself. This means judging anyone in anyway on appearances means you will have to take accountability for that one day.

The physical limitations can make it challenging for someone to break through human superficiality and get into the soul of another person. Only an accelerated soul can get in there and be able to see who someone is. It's being able to see the true soul of the cruelest man. That's not a task that the ego has any interest in. When you judge on the surface, then you can't protest to know about love. Being unable to see the truth and soul of the most difficult person destroys your own spirit.

Love is the most powerful vibration that exists throughout all of time and space. One of the reasons that many don't show love on Earth is because to show love takes effort. Showing hatred is easy, but love...that's something else entirely. Love will always cost you something, whether that's time or energy. Love will cost you pride when you need to not let your ego dominate and let certain things go that someone else did.

Many experience difficulties in the world. Maybe your situation is financial, or you've lost your job and need another job. The good news is God knows it. He knew it before you ever entered into that struggle and He has your big break on His mind, which is all part of the plan for you. Things that happen to you might surprise you, but your Spirit team is never surprised. Like God, they you, know you, care about you, and will come through any struggle and challenge thrown at you. Never give up on life, because you are loved in a way that is bigger than your problems.

Many shun deepening their soul and consciousness through spiritual and religious studies coupled with hard driven life experiences. What good is life if the three components of body, mind, and soul that make up basic healthy survival are ignored and discarded.

Your emotional and mental well-being state is important for numerous reasons. When you're happy and healthy, then the more love and abundance you attract in. This also raises your vibration, which awakens your intuitive psychic connection with Spirit. It is that connection which helps you receive divinely guided information and inspiration designed to keep you on the right path towards soul enlightenment and beyond.

Others have also purported to say they found

that happiness in a strong spiritual connection, whether that is a connection with Jesus, Buddha, God, the Universe, or Spirit. It doesn't matter what you call it even though in some spiritual circles they may do their best to make you feel guilty or bad, and might even bully you for not following who they personally follow.

General spiritual practitioners preach that you be all love and light. If every person on the planet exuded that state, then there would no doubt be peace on Earth.

Since this is not a realistic or practical request that the billions of people on the planet are capable of following, we have to examine this on a deeper realistic level. In the coming chapters we'll look at all things connected to love, which includes spiritual soul love, self-love, as well as physical love such as dating and relationships, which is something of major interest for so many people.

CHAPTER TWO

Creating the Life You Love

Ultimate authentic success surrounds your soul's growth and evolving process. It's when you realize that none of the physical ego driven desires matter in the end. You can work hard to make sure you stay afloat, you're able to pay your bills, and support yourself and family, but you're not chasing friends, likes, followers, fans, or people to prop you up. Any amount of goodness displayed from your heart is the true measure of real accomplishment. An overflowing feeling of optimism and love coupled with faith and action is what increases the chances of attracting good things and positive loved filled experiences to you.

This is a physical world that requires money to survive on this planet. It's misguided to believe that money isn't everything. It is true that money is not everything compared to love, great health, and good loyal friends that understand you and have your back, but the reality is that money is required to survive on the planet. Find that steady balance where you gracefully thrive to achieve to make enough money to be comfortable enough where you no longer have worry of not being able to pay your bills. At the same time avoid getting too carried away with it that you fall into greed territory, which is an abundance killer.

Abundance is more than monetary and financial increase. It can also be about reaching an awe-inspiring optimistic heavenly well-being state of joy, peace, and love. This positive emotional mindful state simultaneously attracts in blessings.

It is not immoral to desire to live securely enough where you have a comfortable place to live, a career, job, and/or hobbies that fulfill you. Your bills get paid without worry and you have a love partner or a healthy social circle. When you're taken care of with your physical needs, then it is easier to focus on what others need. When you feel safe and secure, then your vibration is raised within that comfy nest. This makes you a joy to be around and a powerful abundance love magnet at the same time.

If you desire to buy your own house one day, then begin the visualization of having this house. You can close your eyes at least once a day and envision what this house will look like. You'll visualize its surroundings, the kinds of neighbors that are around you, the location, and everything about it. You'll then visualize yourself living in this house, walking around throughout it, sleeping in your bed in this house, making a meal in the kitchen, the kinds of friends you have visiting this house, or the love partner that is with you in this house and so on. Notice your feelings and state of mind and how you'll feel while living in this house as this is happening.

You can apply this visualization exercise to whatever you desire, whether it's a love relationship, job, car, or anything you long for. This is pending it is aligned with your higher self's purpose and God's will. The benefits to this visualization exercise are that it programs your mind to move away from the doubts and fears that you'll attract this in. It also assists in getting the positive energy surrounding this visualization towards making it happen.

Bring in what you desire by allowing it to flow towards you naturally. You're not chasing your dreams in a panic. You're taking productive action steps through methodical movements with love to obtain what you long for. If there's someone you're interested in romantically, then ask them out whether or not you're male or female. Regardless of their answer, don't chase or burden them by staying on top of them relentlessly. When it's the right one, it will flow and merge with you naturally and organically. Placing any kind of demands will push it away. The same goes for work related endeavors or anything you have your eyes set on.

The serious relationships I've had over the course of my life all transpired without effort. It came to be when I wasn't looking or longing for one. I was in a perfect state of contentment desiring nothing. When I was frustrated or in a negative mindset, then nothing came to pass.

When spreading yourself too thin, you want to ensure to be extra careful about what you're putting into your body. You might complain you're too tired or don't have enough time or energy to contribute up to an hour a day into what could potentially be your full-time job. This is a dilemma and a block for you, but if this is work you truly love, then it doesn't feel like work. It's something you enjoy doing so working on it is rarely a problem. When someone cheerfully wants to do something, then they will do it no matter how tired they are. Putting in efforts towards your passion and love gives you a positive lift, an energy boost, and raises your vibration. All of which are ingredients in that recipe for attracting in positive circumstances, love energy, and abundance.

Raising your vibration is a crucial element in giving you greater love energy and a brighter mood. This encourages you to make the time to contribute towards the things you love. Even after a long day at work at what you might consider to be a day job, when you have more energy, then that's energy to help push you to contribute towards work that you love. Putting love into your work counts as part of the love feelings you are utilizing from within. Love applies to your passions, endeavors and purposes. When you enjoy doing something, then you are putting love energy into it. This expands that love energy making a great deal more.

The reason you might be exhausted at the end of each day is not always because work is so tough at your day job, but it's because this job does not excite you on any level. When you experience excitement, then the feel-good chemical dopamine is released into your system. When you despise what you do, then this depletes the dopamine chemical, which sucks the life force love feeling energy right out of you.

When I'm doing what I love, then the energy keeps going for hours where I don't want to stop. It's a perpetual rushed excited high, because I'm doing what I love that it doesn't feel like work. It's fun and I'm getting paid for it too! On top of that, I'm being extra careful with what I put in my body and system. You know that if you have a glass of wine or a beer in the middle of the day, then you're unlikely to put in any work into what you love.

Human beings have been trained and taught to accumulate material and physical gratification over anything else. Thriving to create and produce what you love is one positive element to abundance, but this is about the obsession to achieve more finances. Chasing a dollar to have more money you do nothing positive with is not a goal to thrive for, but squeezes any love energy right out of you.

For some it becomes hyper mania to obtain additional finances even though they are already financially comfortable enough for life. If there are any positives to chasing finances, then it is to improve the quality of life for yourself, which subsequently enables you to be free to help others. This might be done through things like humanitarian work, charity giving, or you have a staff to employ and need to take care of. By that turn, you're ensuring the survival of more than one person that relies on that paycheck to pay their bills. You are showering love to others by this act. At the same time, chasing anything pushes it further away from you. It's the nature of the way energy attraction tends to operate.

The soul has the capacity to absorb a wealth of knowledge. It has the power to bring in what it desires into its current reality. This starts with a thought, a dream, and a foresight that begins to grow and expand into an intensified crystal-clear vision. What many are longing or fighting for in this human jungle is a profusion of love and abundance.

The traits of happiness and love are traits that every soul on the planet personally longs for. It's become a struggle for many to reach that state of love happiness. They wind up chasing after butterflies and mirages that appear to be enticing as the answer to revealing these riches. The density of the Earth's atmosphere places enormous pressure on the soul that causes communication blockages with the Divine. It messes and tampers with your emotions in trying to find that centered space of peace where you have everything you could ever want. You spend your entire life pursuing those pretty dreams hoping and praying for some blessing or miracle. The answer is in your hand, in your mind, and in your feelings. It is in your soul burning like a raging fire screaming to make that Divine connection where you are transcended into an authentic feeling of joy, love, and peace.

True abundance is living an existence where you are functioning in the highest soul love vibration possible. You are filled with God and Spirit's love. It is overflowing to the point that you experience upbeat high vibrational emotions. It is impractical in today's world to be in that state non-stop every second, even though you can imagine how awesome life would be if that were humanly possible. Many attempt to artificially create that feeling through toxins.

If everyone followed the mantra of functioning without stress, obscenity-ridden judgments, and instead chose to live in a joyful peaceful compassionate state, then this would be a utopian paradise. This is unlikely to happen anytime soon. Especially considering that the planet is centuries and more into humanity's progression and life on Earth, and yet the globe is still unable to revert to love as the core manner of communicating with others. Discord has been ripe with relentless fury since the first human beings walked the Earth. It has never lightened up.

Humanity has a tough time in thinking and feeling in love. This isn't about being 100% positive 24/7, as that is an impossible feat even if your general disposition is a happy content positive one. It does mean going back to the mantra that if you don't have anything nice to say, then don't say anything. When you're experiencing negative or challenging anything, then take the time to move through that. Examine what it is that took place in your life that threw your world off kilter.

CHAPTER THREE

Self-Love and Self-Care

You must love yourself first before you can faithfully love another person. It might seem to be there is quite a bit of self-love going on in places like social media, but when you're posting content with the ultimate goal of gaining accolades, comments, likes, and followers, then that is the opposite of authentic self-love. It is placing the responsibility on other people to fill you up with the kind of love that no human being can give. You are reaching out to external sources to boost your self-esteem, which is never permanently successful.

There are endless studies and statistics that have indicated how social media has crumbled one's wholeness and well-being state. There have also been numerous interviews of some of the world's popular social media influencers that have admitted to the depressing loneliness they experience. They've illustrated that their social media accounts give people the false illusion that they're popular due to the one million followers they have, but if they were in a personal crisis there is no one around them they can truly call a friend.

This is because the kind of love the soul part of you is attempting to grasp is reachable within you. This is where the Divine source of love is that lifts you up into the heavens while raising your vibration and consciousness. It is the source of true authentic love that increases your self-esteem, self-love and independence from the toxic addiction of relying on external sources for this impossible love.

One of the ways to find this kind of love is to practice self-love and self-care. It is paying attention to what you need rather than what others can give you. The more you raise your self-love awareness, then the more opened up your world will become. There is no telling what you can accomplish and attract in when you have built up that inner confidence through this act of self-love.

Participating in self-love and self-care means to also give you personal time. This is a much-needed intermission your soul needs regular amounts of in order to recharge and decompress from the stresses of the physical life. It is time devoted to you alone or with a loved one. When you're alone sitting in a park, in meditation, or in nature somewhere, you're able to clear your mind and allow perspective and additional Divinely guided ideas to flow into your soul without any physical distractions. It is what fills your soul up with the love you've been struggling and fighting to get from external sources. You gather up the newly gained incoming ammunition and tools and store it away for future use. This is when you re-emerge from your personal soul time and back into the next phase of your physical world action momentum. You take the tools and knowledge gained from this personal soul time and apply it towards your next new chapter of forward motion. Practicing self-love and self-care enables you to accomplish your life purposes. You take your time and enjoy what you're doing without the desire for external praise and adoration.

You're not intended to have a miserable life. Pleasures and playtime fun are essential are all part of self-love and self-care. One of its necessary functions is that it ensures you are not overloaded with constant stress on your body and overall health. Self-love and self-care are necessities that prevent you from experiencing burnout. This isn't about the kinds of pleasures that are considered toxic, dangerous, or unhealthy. It might be to go on a hike with a friend, or a fun road trip to a destination far enough away from home to feel as if you're getting away, but close enough to get to. Give yourself enough time to take regular breaks and see places you've always wanted to visit and explore. It can be watching a movie that entertains, inspires, and helps you escape a hard circumstance for a time period. It can be spending intimate time with a lover, a best friend, your pet or family member. Giving to you is part of self-love and self-care. By taking time out of your busy life to play has many positive health and success benefits.

Self-love includes loving all that you are. It is to love and accepts how you look, which is something many suffer from including those that you wouldn't think to be the case. Those that primarily post one photo of themselves after another are seeking love or praise from others. This isn't about the occasional photo one posts, but rather those that crave external validation and approval. This includes those who appear hot in the eyes of others. I've seen some posters post one hot photo of themselves after another with some inspiring words. They either likely know that is what will attract in praise and followers, or they are seeking external approval and validation.

The ones that aren't seeking that out are the ones that unsurprisingly are not as popular when it comes to social media domination. They're not playing the game of approval seeking, which is what attracts in popularity. The ego in humankind is attracted to pretty people with beautiful sayings. In mythology it was Narcissus who saw his hot sexy reflection in a pool of water and fell in love with himself. Due to this extreme form of self-love he ended up killing himself because he could not attain that person in the reflection. This is a symbolic metaphor for human behavior on social media today.

With anything in life, you want to keep it balanced and in moderation. This goes for self-love where you give yourself just enough self-love acceptance where it raises your self-esteem, but isn't pushed past that breaking point into narcissism, because then you've aligned yourself with the Narcissist that fell in love with his own reflection that it caused his demise. What you might perceive to be a flaw in your appearance is subjective. Even the hottest person on the planet isn't attractive to every single person that exists. Most everyone I've ever talked to has opened up about what they feel is their flaw. This includes from those that you would think have people lined up outside their door because of how good-looking they are. I've heard those same good-looking people tell me random things out of nowhere that they perceive as a flaw. Things like, "My nose is too big." Or "My ears are too small."

These are things that no one notices in the way they do. They see what they feel is a problem about themselves and they magnify it to the point of extremism.

Learn to love everything about you flaws and all without the need for external approval. Change the things you're able to change about yourself that you feel could use an adjustment. Love and accept the areas that you know you will never be able to improve. The things that you perceive to be as flaws are qualities that God loves about you. All heavenly spirit beings see you as pure love inside and out. They have a hard time grasping why so many people spend each day longing for constant validation and approval that will never come no matter how hard they try. It feels like an exhausting way to live inside one's head demanding that endless craving of love and adoration that comes from above, not from human beings.

Where can it get you to sit around all day thinking low thoughts about yourself one after the other? Love yourself because you are created in His image. You were born out of this love from the creator who loves you unconditionally. Those negative words you tell yourself are untrue in the eyes of Heaven. They seem or feel true from your own current reality and perception, but not in the eyes of God. Many that seek out this external love do it in frustration only to be met with disappointment. They are usually people that don't have a higher profound faithful spirit belief and connection, which is why they chase human beings for it down here. Your soul is perfection in every way loved unconditionally for all that you are, including your strengths and what you consider to be personal flaws. Love, accept, and appreciate you, because you're a gift!

External human validation isn't something I require, because I know my worth through God. I know who I am, what I can do, and what I've done. Believe in yourself and give yourself credit when you do good things. Praising yourself is considered self-love that lifts your vibration up into the vortex of attracting in more good stuff.

Most people are only super close to a few others in person that you can count on one or both of your hands. Everyone else outside of that is extended friends, family, or acquaintances. These are people that you are friendly with when you bump into one another, but they don't necessarily know about every shred you're going through on a daily basis the way the super close ones do. Authentic love comes from those that know everything about you and are still with you. They never criticize you, but support you and stand by you as you do with them. You both know how to give this love authentically.

Someone might have hundreds of acquaintances, business associates, and appear to be super popular in person or on social media, but in the end the super close ones that know every shred of breath they utter are on the minimal side. Those people are the ones that would be there during your most dire of circumstances. They stand by you when you're at your best as well as your worst. They are the ones that have your back while supporting your endeavors. They will offer constructive criticism, which you can handle if you're headed for a cliff you cannot see. In the end, what matters is the quality of people around you and not the quantity.

This is also true for those people with thousands of likes on their social media accounts. I have friends who are exceptional masters on social media with the tens of thousands and millions of followers and likes, yet knowing them in person they have a small number of quality friendships that know the real deal and day-to-day nitty-gritty happenings going on with them behind closed doors.

This is also true for well-known celebrities or public figures who have followers and likes in the hundreds of thousands and on up into the millions. Knowing some of them in my personal life I can tell you that they are no different than any other friend. In the end, they are surrounded by a small number of quality people in the real-life reality outside of the media platforms. They are not as big as the public believes them to be in their personal life.

The media and social media recycle this false deception to the public. Even if you're unknown to the world, you choose what you decide to post on your social media. It's never enough for anyone to know the real you because you're controlling what is out there. It's all an illusion and you have to be careful not to get swept up in that fiction believing this is the way to obtain love.

It might seem as if some are more loved than others, but popularity is an illusion because the love you think they're receiving is a superficial one. People may love that person's work or the way they look, but they don't know who that person is deep down on a daily and regular basis. Will they be by their bedside upon death's door?

Perhaps you long for strangers to like you. You will do anything to grab that adoration, idolatry, and admiration. Who cares if anyone likes you? Focus on your purpose and don't worry so much about being propped up by others. Lean on Spirit, God, and Heaven in order to prop yourself up and stay focused on what needs to be accomplished while on your path.

Some people might reach a higher popularity than someone else making it seem as if they're more worthy of popularity, but popularity doesn't matter in the end. No one will remember much about anyone presently popular one hundred years from now.

What is in your heart and what you set out to do is what matters. If your heart and soul is bathed in negativity and hatred, then your soul light is a flicker ready to go out leaving you in darkness. The popularity is insincere and fleeting on Earth. Someone outwardly unpopular on Earth is in actuality more popular in spiritual soul reality if what they put out into the world is authentic.

Your strength and gifts are much needed to help move humanity through the next transition and into the next plateau. Make good with your intentions, follow through, take action, cut out those that are perpetually negative, bullying, or abusive. None of the noise around you is important. What is important is your character, your soul's true nature, and what you intend to accomplish while here. Stay focused on the job at hand, but also remember to inject regular breaks, fun, and relaxation. Your soul will always thank you for those gifts of leisure. It makes you that much stronger and ready to forge forward fearlessly after having rested up and re-charged.

Current human life has propelled others to become obsessed by youth and exterior appearances. For some it is to the point where reality has fazed those that have fallen into the epicenter of this superficiality. There was a time pre-technology days when you respected your elders. Now many disrespect those older because they are ageist and under the delusion they are untouchable and exempt from aging. Popular culture in Entertainment became more about visual appearances in the music industry, rather than making and playing great music. Magazines airbrushed their models and celebrities almost to the point of making them unrecognizable in some cases. Even the most amateur photographer on the planet that enjoys taking their daily selfies will ensure that the filters are just right. The photos must appear attractive enough to post for validation and praise. This all stems from the soul's core desire of longing to be loved, admired, and praised. Many desire this deep down, but some take it to the furthest extreme more than others.

Some desire praise and attention more than others to the degree of extremism. They cannot help it because they desire and crave admiration and love. A soul was born out of love and will die right back into that love. It moves about in a human body longing to be hugged, cuddled, and loved up. When that love is starved from their existence, then they may harden and toughen up, become distant, aloof, cold and indifferent. Or they may head in the opposite direction and compensate by trying anything and everything to find ways to gain that praise and admiration that never sticks. It only lasts for a millisecond until they notice that people have moved onto other things and no longer have any interest in them again. It's dangerous to place your well-being state in the hands of others. Relying on people online and around you to continuously prop you up and feel good about yourself can become tiresome from all aspects. Love yourself and all that you are now.

The body is temporary, and it is aging each day

until it stops working and ultimately disintegrates as your soul leaves it and soars into the other world. This scares some causing them to be unsure of what happens after that. They may believe there is life after death or they're hesitant because they don't see it with their own eyes. The one thing everyone agrees on is that we will all cease to live on this planet forever. Those that invested deeply into the physical material world may have the greatest fear involved. The reality check will hit them on their deathbed when the material fades away.

As you grow older, you want to reach the realization that you don't have a choice and you have to strengthen your faith and resolve. This is partially why you may have noticed that as one grows older their spiritual belief system seems to become stronger. This is the case even if they were a non-believer in younger age. Perhaps they won't suddenly believe in God, but they will grow more open minded of the possibilities of something good beyond their Earthly life. They subconsciously know that their body will permanently stop working for good. It will shut down and become lifeless. They may hopefully see that their soul and consciousness is somewhere in there and that it will continue on. The struggle for likes, followers, and praise suddenly appears trivial in comparison to what is coming up for every single person on the planet.

The human bodies were not designed to live forever. You reach older age signified by your physical body aging, and eventually shutting down.

The body will die, and the soul will exit and move on to new destinies. There is no way around that. No one would want to live on this planet forever since back home is where the true fun and serenity exists full time. You are with those in your soul tribe, whereas on Earth you are mixed in with all souls in various levels of growth. Many souls in a human body use enormous amounts of dark ego, which dominates their higher self. This is what causes so much unrest, a lack of love, and unhappiness on the planet. The ever growing and expanding spiritual metaphysical movement has been helping to make one another's souls more aware, conscious, and enlightened about life beyond the physical and superficial. The goal of spirit is to bring all into the highest vibrational love state possible around the globe, so that Heaven can exist on Earth.

Other ways of inviting more self-love is not only giving to yourself, but it includes giving to others. It is also about receiving from others in the right spirit. Give and receive throughout the course of your day-to-day movements in order to increase the balance of feelings of self-love and Universal love. Giving is not necessarily giving money away, although giving something to your favorite charities counts. Giving is also the giving of a small positive act to another person that has the potential to brighten their day, such as a smile or a compassionate complimentary word or more.

Sometimes it's the little acts of kindness that might go unnoticed, but which are actually creating a wave of love. One person makes one small kind move to help someone, then that person carries that act of love and compassion to another, and so on until it wraps back around reaching the original person again in the end.

What you put out eventually comes back to you. This is seen on the planet with the dark energy, but rarely shown are these small moments of love from others in the seemingly smallest of ways. I notice those little small acts of kindness from others that come through out of that one amazing person out of hundreds.

Once I had dropped a huge wad of cash not realizing it. This guy jogged after me and said, "Excuse me."

I turned around and he had a smile, "You dropped this, here you go."

I said stunned, "What? Thank you. Wait a minute, who does what you just did?"

I handed him some of it as a reward.

He put his hand up refusing it and said, "Just pay it forward."

I smiled, "I will."

Another incident, I was standing at a urinal and this guy tapped me and said, "I think this is yours."

It was my driver's license. These things might be small, but you'd be surprised how rare those small acts of kind gestures are. There are people with ill intentions that might steal it, throw it away, or not bother to say anything.

At one point in my life, I ended up on crutches for six weeks after tearing the tendon on my foot during a bootleg camp work out accident where I landed on a jump wrong. Everything is fine today as if it never happened, but back then I was balancing on the crutches and putting groceries into my car with another hand. This well-to-do rich woman in her thirties with one of those massive SUV's was loading up her car before she caught my juggling act. Like a fireman answering a bell she gasped and quickly jogged over to me to help. Again, you'd be surprised that those little things are rare, so when they happen you do feel the magic of humanity's compassion that is in there deep down.

Use God's mantra of remembering to spread more love, more kindness, and more compassion, even in those tiny gestures like a smile to a stranger. They add up and do mean something in the eyes of God and the Universal energy. You don't do those things for fanfare or attention, nor to get something in return. You do it because you have a strong willed compassionate sensitive part of you that cares wanting to be of service. In Heaven, all spirit beings want to be of service. They don't have the massive dark egos that human beings have where there often seems to be an ulterior motive that isn't aligned with the soul's higher good.

Being of service are the little gestures that are actually large blessings you're giving to other people. It doesn't take much to brighten someone's day just from a simple move. Because there isn't enough of it as it is, that when it does happen, whoever is on the receiving end notices it.

I've had people tell me that only one person smiled at them throughout the day, and it was that one person that stood out enough that it uplifted their energy after that. They could feel it shift just from a stranger's random genuine smile. Sometimes those reminders are God working through other people to reach out and make that positive move towards someone that could use it at that moment.

Give yourself a break from the struggles in life and practice the joy and love you can feel from receiving. Many spiritual or compassionate people have the qualities of being a selfless giver. While this is a magnificent heavenly trait to have, you can create an imbalance when that is all you are doing. In order to bring balance into your life, be open to receive in your life as well. When someone wants to do something nice for you for a change, then welcome that with open arms. Those who are predominately givers tend to wrestle with the joy of receiving. They might fall into the category of someone taking advantage of them. Never mistake kindness for weakness.

Receiving is also giving to yourself where you are the receiver, which is part of self-love and self-care. It's treating yourself to something you love such as a weekend getaway somewhere or a spa day if you enjoy being pampered. Whatever it is that makes you smile to receive, then go for it and give to yourself regularly to increase your self-love and self-esteem.

CHAPTER FOUR

Karmic Soul Connections

After you've mastered the art of regularly incorporating self-love, then you are ready to move into the world of relationships. From a young age, I had quickly begun the process of studying the human condition as well as the various relationship dynamics that exist between others. I can remember being a love bug Don Juan Casanova type from as far back as five years old when I recall developing my first crush. I've spent a great deal of my life experimenting and experiencing every kind of relationship dynamic possible, including but not limited to witnessing my parents own Karmic Relationship to the deep Soul Mate love relationships I've had that were filled with the kind of love you find in a romantic novel or movie. I've also experienced my own personal Karmic Relationships with less than suitable partners when I was in my twenties. These were partners I had intended to marry at the time; therefore, you can understand how deep each and every love relationship partner I've had has been romantic, passionate, and intense. It comes with the territory when you're with me. As I grew older, my partners grew more stable as did I. Hence, the karma was being balanced out to the point that there were virtually no real major issues in the latter relationships and years of my life.

You romantically dream it up and I likely experienced it from the kissing in the rain to the cathedral like set up when getting proposed to. Love has been my overall nature and it stays locked up only displaying it on those trustworthy enough for that kind of intensity.

In my late teens and early twenties, I started writing column pieces on love, dating, sex, and relationships. That became the genre I primarily chose to gravitate towards and focus on. I've also always been in love with love. I've been around the block my friends have said. This is through the life course of studying, reading and psychically scanning others that pass me, while avoiding anyone that I pick up on as dangerous, while welcoming in those that are filled with love.

There has no doubt been a rise in a great dividing intolerant wave of hatred that is completely devoid of love around the globe. There is no Light and no psychic intuition in that space. I've been versed in the nature of soul connections since I was born and understand it all well. This is because like you, I am a child of God. I'm also a Warrior of Light, a channel for the Divine, a lifelong psychic and medium. Since I was four years old, my focus has primarily been aimed at the Light. The endless exactitudes I've protested over the course of my life have led myself and my Spirit team to discuss the truths and mythology over some of the spiritual concepts made popular over the years. This includes karmic relationships, soul mates, and twin flames. Some believe in all of those things, some of those things, or neither of those things. Regardless if one believes it or not, we're going to use those terms in the coming chapters for the sake of easily identifying the differences. Irrespective of what it's called they are some of the varying soul connections that exist on Earth.

This planet is still having a tough time moving into that love space after all these centuries of Earth's evolution. In the end, your soul's life was born out of love and it will die right back into that love. Love is the only power that can kill the demon, the ego, the devil, and the darkness in one big bang.

You could possibly be part of the many around the planet that have been in the kind of love relationship that transcends time and space. This love lifts you up into the Heavens and transports you to places you never thought possible to reach. It's a mutual deep physical attraction sensed upon first sight with another person. Before you know it, you're dating and quickly falling into an immediate love connection. You've been waiting for this your entire life and now it's real and in motion. Life couldn't be any better!

As your relationship connection continues through its initial beginning stages, your intensity for this person never wanes, but instead grows to an obsession. This is the one you've been waiting for without a doubt in your mind, because no other relationship has been this intense before. You've finally found that love paradise that artists write about in romantic novels, films, and songs. This is the honeymoon period of a love connection.

The honeymoon period in a love connection is the initial beginning stages of two people coming together romantically. The honeymoon period can last from one week to around eighteen months. This is before the honeymoon blush begins to gradually wear off if it hadn't already by that point.

After the blush has dissolved, then that is the moment when both partners begin to know if the relationship is truly working or not. Most relationships have a hard time making it to the end of that period, which has been made clear through endless statistics being polled. The couple will be hot and heavy the first few weeks to a few months upon meeting before watching the connection dismantle. One or the both of them realize that now that the newness has subsided they're actually not that into the other person as much as they thought.

It's a testy time for relationships in general. Most relationships today have a challenging time lasting until death do either of you part. If you are one of the exceptions at this point, then treasure what you have to the greatest of your ability, because you have what many either long for or are incapable of sustaining.

If someone is physically attractive, then the relationship might last a bit longer due to the lust filled magnetism had with the attractive person. You're not necessarily truly compatible with the person you have a physical attraction for, but because you find them physically attractive you're pulled in for longer than it should've been. Being with a physically attractive person is like witnessing a beautiful butterfly flitting around you. That person can do no wrong when you've got those rose-colored glasses on. Look at how society puts attractive people on a pedestal just for looking good. They treat them with more love and compassion than someone they don't find attractive or see to be average. Attractive people surmount a huge amount of likes and followers, even though they're not really selling a product except endless selfies. Beyond physical attraction there is no other chemistry to keep the connection cemented and enduring.

If you've fallen into the drunken hazy love of that kind of adoration for someone way too good looking, then you need great will power to take a higher step back to truly examine if they're a good person for you or not. Are you brushing aside certain behavior traits they do that you normally wouldn't be so forgiving with if it were someone else?

Enormous deception is the challenge of walking into the beginning stages of a bright new love connection. One day you wake up to find the relationship has abruptly broken apart. You wonder how this is possible as you were sure this person was the one.

One of the two in the partnership starts to display an eerie disinterest that builds causing them to pull away or ultimately walk away from the connection. This leaves you with this dark heavy pain that burdens your heart and simultaneously places a huge weight on your soul. Some justify the reasoning the partner left being due to the runner part of the runner chaser equation theory pushed in twin flame circles. It's the only way to help you make sense of why the person you thought could be the love of your life turned their back on your comfortable love nest. You cannot understand how this could happen because this person was supposed to be the one.

The intense love feelings were there, but those intense love feelings are present for most every deep romantic love connection in the beginning stages. Your feelings cannot always be trusted when you fall in love with someone. Falling in love puts you into a joyful happy place, but it also places rosy glasses over your psychic visions. Suddenly all of the rules are thrown out the window and Divine instincts are reduced. This evidence is present and all around through the millions of deep intense love relationships that break apart sooner than later causing the person that was blindsided to note that in hindsight the red flags were there, but they chose to ignore them. They believed their mate was the one to the degree that the infatuation carried them away on that love causing them to brush any practical sense aside.

Since most relationships have trouble lasting until the end of their days, the odds of it being a twin flame connection will be slim. An authentic twin flame soul connection tends to last indefinitely. We say it tends to because there are rare cases that a twin flame relationship will break apart and stay apart. The truth is the relationship just described at the start of this scenario was actually a Karmic Relationship.

Karmic Relationships

Every soul on the planet is developing and creating karma every day through their actions, thoughts, and deeds. Karma is being created quickly with the relationships you have with others including friendships, family members, business colleagues and lovers. We're focusing on the love-oriented relationships in this example, but it can be applied to other types of connections as well too.

Karmic relationships can start off exceptionally deep and intense. God and your Spirit team bring the two souls together in a radiant attractive enticing shower bathed in enormous intensity. This is to make the two inseparable for the purpose of balancing out past karma. If they have an intense draw to one another, then they are more than likely going to come together to take care of soul business. If there is no intensity, then it is unlikely to draw them in, thus leaving the karmic pattern stuck on pause. They come together intensely until they are no longer inseparable and the restraints they formed have been broken. The connection and interest in one another begin to dissolve.

What happened was the karmic thread had completed and been balanced out. There was nothing left to learn with this person. If the person comes back, then that could mean the connection had not balanced out the karmic thread completely the first time around. Usually a partner will come back at another time allowing the opportunity for both people to balance out the Karma and produce healing, which is then followed by official closure.

You will know that the karmic relationship is complete when you have both moved on your separate ways. You have no negative thoughts or feelings about them. This means any previous animosity, anger, or sadness attributed to thoughts or feelings about them have dissolved, or they've been significantly reduced you hardly notice it anymore. You are in a place of peace and contentment with the fact that you are no longer in that partnership anymore. There is no feeling of something missing after they've gone. In fact, you don't care whether or not they come back. You are open to new experiences and relationships.

All souls are developing, creating, mending, and balancing out karma. Whenever you come into contact with someone and have any kind of relationship, then you are both creating karma due to the actions on both of your parts. Karmic relationships may start off amazingly hot and heavy, but eventually they tend to be bathed in some kind of turmoil, drama, or chaos. Some are more extreme in this than others.

Many karmic relationships are displayed in all its nonsense and glory on social media or in the media. This is because the public's dark ego receives a rushed high over drama and watching the theatrical lives of others. Dramatic and chaotic relationships love to use the world as its stage. This is also why tabloids became a billion-dollar enterprise. It's why reality television and reality stars were propelled to celebrity status. It was due to the public's obsession with drama fueling all of that to the top of the charts.

There is no God or spiritual essence in drama, because that is where the darkness of ego resides. Every person on the planet has had or will have a karmic relationship with someone else, whether it be a friendship, colleague, neighbor, love connection, and so on. There is no limit to the dynamic that the relationship will form.

Karmic connections can be a soul mate partnership as well too. The difference is that soul mates are not perpetually antagonistic. They might have the occasional antagonism, but not to the daily or weekly degree that a karmic relationship does.

Soul mate partnerships are a give and take, whereas a karmic relationship tends to mostly be a taking kind of relationship. It's always about me or what you're not doing for me. Karmic partnerships tend to complain incessantly about their partner with anyone who will listen.

The karmic soul partner may show up in the beginning putting on the act of a chivalrous Prince or Princess, but as the connection grows you begin to notice little red flags popping up. You may eventually believe them to be sociopathic or narcissistic. These red flags are those warning signs that something is not right. You might brush off the first few red flags. Some will even brush off the first few dozen red flags, but their friends won't. Someone's good soul mate friendships tend to see that this relationship is a problem long before you do. You don't see the love relationship the same way they do because anybody you're romantically connected with is the world to you. You're just happy as a clam to be entangled with someone in a love connection that you'll accept the drama over being alone.

Millions of souls crave love and companionship, which is why they seek out committed love relationships with one another. Everyone has challenges they endure and there will be trials no matter how spiritual or put together you are.

Karmic relationships end up being the ones wrecked with some kind of negativity, drama, or endless challenges. There are more people in karmic relationships today than in any other kind of relationship. This is partly due to the ego driven modern day world that life on Earth has become. It's a me-first attitude and this is taught in almost every circle. If someone doesn't get what they want, then they throw a tantrum, or they take to the streets or social media to protest and complain. There is no love in any of that space. What you have is new karma being created. The positive that comes out of that are lessons and potential soul growth. Having a genuine love relationship requires sacrifice and compromise.

Because there are more karmic relationships than any other kind of relationship, then that means that many karmic relationships have been mistaken to be twin flame connections. Some may explain away that their twin flame turned out to be a narcissus, which is unlikely to be the case. It's not that twin soul flames are above or below being a narcissus, but the odds of the twin flame being a narcissus is on the slim side. This is due to the twin flame having evolved more rapidly on their soul's path in terms of spiritual growth that succumbing to narcissism is also rare. If they do fall into some narcissistic tendencies, then it's so miniscule compared to others that it's almost never a problem.

The narcissus terminology gained steam when social media, technology, and the Internet took off. Many will use the sociopath or narcissistic word if someone leaves them, but they do not truly understand its psychological definition. Because in its definition most everyone can be accused of vacillating between the humble to narcissistic on any given day. If a partner was indeed a narcissus based on the psychological definition, then they were more than likely in a karmic relationship.

CHAPTER FIVE

Soul Mate
Soul Connections

Heaven understands the negative challenges that people are assaulted with on a regular basis. No one is exempt from challenges, because if you don't have challenges, then you don't grow. Your individual Spirit team works to assist in bringing soul mates into your life with the goal of assisting you in various ways while on your journey here. One soul mate might have one purpose to accomplish with you, while another will have several. Some of them help out by offering mutual support as you endure these challenges.

These people are called Soul Mates. The word

soul describes the part of you that is separate from your body. When you pass onto the Other Side, your soul exits your body, and your physical body disintegrates into dust, but your soul and consciousness carry on and move onto other destinies in the next plane back home.

Mate can mean a love partner, a companion, a friend, or a business associate. It is a pair of two people joining together for a purpose or purposes. This would be someone who is comparable to you. Soul mates are other souls you cross paths with for a specific purpose or purposes that are aligned with teaching or learning something from this person and vice versa. Everyone has something to teach one another and learn from, even if it's not evident at first.

Soul mates can be a lover, a friend, a work colleague, a pet, a parent, a sibling, a neighbor, an acquaintance, or even someone you crossed paths with for several minutes. This might be someone that says a profound line to you in a quick conversation that makes you think or propels you to make a positive change in your life.

Perhaps you strike up a conversation with a stranger in an elevator. During that short ride that stranger manages to say something that makes you think about something in a deeper way. Sometimes the stranger can act as a catalyst that prompts you to action. Often a spirit guide or angel will have other soul mates deliver messages to you in this way. The soul mate will offer you challenges to overcome that enable your soul to grow and evolve.

A soul mate friend will pull you out of your

comfort zone and toss the metaphorical ball to you to take and run with it. Your guardian spirit is right there on the field coaxing you both along to be proactive in your life.

When you evolve out of karmic relationships and into selflessness in love, then you are moving into what you can do for your partner and vice versa. This is when you have a greater opportunity to graduate into healthier soul mate partnerships. Healthy soul mate partnerships praise and uplift their partner, rather than complain or beat them down. This also means it's a mutual reciprocation, because if you're always doing something for a partner who doesn't reciprocate that, then that's called co-dependency which is an imbalance.

Co-dependency can point to a lack of self-love, therefore you look to others to receive that love and become co-dependent on it. There may be some that fall into the space of needing constant attention from others, whether it's from a lover, friends, family members, or strangers. They love messages of joy, but fail to notice when they have been guilty of falling into the co-dependency aspect part of it. People cannot fulfill that kind of unrealistic demand from another person.

It's pretty common to seek out attention and love from external sources from the teenage years on up into one's early twenties. One hopes that by the time you begin moving into your late twenties that your desire for external sources to shower you with love begin to fade. You realize that it can be conjured up naturally by standing in your own independent soul power and connecting with the

Divine.

The soul mate will offer you challenges to overcome that enable your soul to grow and evolve. They might be someone that shows up at just the right time it is needed to offer love and support, such as when a parent or child passes on and a soul mate shows up in the form of your pet dog to give you that unconditional devotion and love you crave during that grieving period in your life. Or your best friend calls you regularly to offer cheering support about something. This person is also your soul mate. Your love mate stands by you through this time of grieving. They are also your soul mate. Your soul mate will also push you out of your comfort zone coaxing you to go after someone or something that you are fearful of. They can be someone that happened to show up at the time you needed it in your life most, then they evaporate away.

This might be an acquaintance that temporarily befriended you. You realize they helped you through a tough time in life, but then as you healed the connection dismantled gradually. This is because the purpose was fulfilled. God and your Spirit team are sending soul mates to others for the purpose of guiding them through a tough challenging time in life or for something specific. Once that mission is complete, then the connection becomes moot.

Soul mates are not interested in holding you back or pushing you down. They're typically not abusive, but they may give you tough love. Tough love is someone that may push you out of your comfort zone to get you out there on that stage and display your talents. They may shine the spotlight on both your strengths and challenges or as some call flaws. Their motive is to coax you on to become better than you are now, even though they also see you as perfection in their eyes the way God does. They understand there is always room for anyone to improve. They understand you have dreams and they want to help you go after them, but you are the same way in return for them too. The soul mate friendships in my life helped me become who I am today. When I was in my late teens and early twenties, I was much darker than I am now. You know the look of a punk kid with a skateboard and the dark black hoody over my head. The kind of dark character that Tim Burton would have a field day creating in one of his masterpieces.

One of my soul mate friends who is still around today is a confident physical fitness trainer. He had told me something interesting once when I was in my early twenties. He gave me this long talk that people keep telling him how deep and intense my eyes are. The issue is that I would avoid looking at people or I would hide them behind gigantic dark jet-black sunglasses the way Anna Wintour does. He explained that my eyes are one of my winning cards and that he noticed the moments that my gaze is held on someone he would see them grow intimidated and suddenly melt. He was trying to get me to understand to use my eyes on people more because the effect is so powerful. I had never heard that before, so I decided to practice doing it for fun to see if he was right, and he was. Doors were opening and my world was becoming more successful. I thought how odd all for just doing that one move of using my eyes as weapons so to speak. This soul mate friend indirectly wound up being one of the many that helped me rise up into that warrior confidence that so many comment on today. This story is to illustrate that I wasn't necessarily showing that constant warrior like confidence. It is also explaining how a soul mate is someone that can provide some tiny shred of advice that you take to heart and end up running with it. Think back to those moments when someone said some compassionate words of recommendation that propelled you to incorporate into your life. This is an example of the role of a soul mate. They are unknowingly working through God and Spirit to relay information that they are helping you to do in order to become who you truly are.

Soul mates will not always have something in common with you. This is why some soul mate connections might seem challenging because perhaps one of you is extroverted and the other is introverted. Some introverted souls are rubbed the wrong way when in the presence of an abrasive outgoing soul, while the extroverted soul will feel as if they're working overtime to bring the introverted person out of their shell. When you give the connection a chance, you both discover that you end up admiring this outgoing cheeriness in this extroverted person, while they admire your put together more introspective and creative part of you. These are souls that challenge you in a positive way to open up and come out of your shell, while you enlighten the more outgoing soul. It might at first make you feel uncomfortable, but then as you think about it and remove your ego from the equation you realize that perhaps they might be right.

Soul mates direct your attention towards something or someone in a loving compassionate way. They might be the best friend that has your back and coaxes you to excel in ways that you normally would not have done had you not had that supportive push.

When you have that realization moment in your life that positive changes need to be made, then it is expected that you would pull yourself back up and release that need to give someone else power over you. While it's nice to have that great time with someone else, it's even more profound when you let go of the need to rely on them to prop you up into happiness.

Everyone on the planet comes across dozens of soul mates throughout the course of their lifetime. You might have formed soul mate friendships that were instant simpatico upon meeting. You both knew you were meant to connect with one another. There can be the fleeting soul mate connections where someone showed up just as you needed it most. They might have offered wisdom that helped you move to the next level in your life or helped you get over the pain of an event that left you broken.

Another example of a soul mate is someone that tests you, pushes your buttons, or supports you and teaches you things you hadn't considered before meeting them.

Soul mates can also be people you've never met such as your favorite entertainer, artist, actor, singer, photographer, or writer. The benefit the teacher has as that person's soul mate is passing on wisdom or inspiration through their work, since soul mate relationships happen in order for the purpose of teaching or learning. If someone pushes you to success even if you don't know them personally, then that person acted as a soul mate without realizing it.

Another best friend of over twenty years at this point is one of my many soul mates. He is outgoing and a strong forceful character. He is also someone you don't want to get into it with, as there have been times where he will dominate and win a debate.

When I was talking to a close relative of his about him once I said, "He and I have never got into a fight in all these years."

This relative said matter of fact and with surety, "That's because you two are soul mates."

I had never given it that much thought until that point. The soul mates in my personal life are all around me on a personal level, while I'm simultaneously awakening parts of souls whom I do not know simply through my writing work and teachings. This has been one of my life purposes in that respect. It is to help others be better people, make sounder choices, connect with their Spirit team more efficiently, and to awaken parts of their higher self's soul that may have been asleep for some time. This doesn't mean I'm infallible and without challenges. I too am a constant work in progress and continuously learning through God and the guidance of my own Spirit team. There is no way I would protest to be all knowing since no human being is all knowing. You cannot be your own God. The work my Spirit team and I do is also for me too. If no one cares about our preaching, then I'll preach to myself since the work is helping me grow my consciousness in the process. I've seen my earlier work and cringed while being able to detect that I'm no longer that guy anymore. I've graduated over different levels in the process of the work. It's also a bit eerie and interesting to see that it's all displayed publicly at the same time.

You have many soul mates throughout the duration of your Earthly life. There is no limit or number to the amount of soul mates you will cross paths with. When some think of a soul mate or twin flame, they automatically equate it to a passionate romantic relationship where you're making love on a white sandy palm tree lined beach in paradise for the rest of your lives. This beautiful mythological notion has caused great turmoil in others who long for this person that fits the description of a lothario character in a romance novel. It is also an unrealistic and misguided interpretation of the soul mate and twin flame dynamic.

Clearing up some of the myths while revealing tips on how to recognize these unique soul connections can be somewhat simplified. All human souls desire some measure of unconditional love and attention deep down within including the most jaded and hardened criminal like mind. This admiration craving is a detachment from God. God being the omnipresent energy space that fills up every cell that exists. He breathes life into every space filled in all existence and all dimensions into infinity and beyond. The stronger your Divine connection with the Other Side is, then the closer you are to understanding the true nature of love and love connections.

It's a basic human desire to long for some form of a companionship. It is the deep love connections that many crave more than any other. There are people who would like that friend companionship in one person, but it doesn't necessarily need to be a passionate love connection. In the end, a passionate sexual connection with the same person for life is rare, because even the most passionate couples experience lulls in that department on occasion. This may turn many off insisting that they will never allow that to happen.

That would be beyond your control. The human body ages and develops issues whether physical, emotional, or mental that creates roadblocks cutting off that passionate supply link you have with another person. What matters is the strong bond and companionship you have with that one person. As you age into your senior golden years, what many end up longing for at that point is someone just to have dinner with once in awhile, or perhaps to hold hands gazing out at a sunset perfectly content in one another's spaces. If you're unhappy with your current partner, then there is someone that would be happy to take them off your hands and they will accept your partner as is just to have that companionship.

Your life doesn't have to end as you move into your golden years. Many have announced they've noticed friends have moved away or passed on. This leaves little human contact from someone in the form of a friend. Sex drives and sex interests decline leaving one to experience loneliness or boredom if there are no hobbies or activities that you enjoy filling in those empty spaces. Many desire someone else to fill this missing void that seems to have been extracted from you, yet is alive and well deep inside burning like the embers on a log. You may be like me - a romantic at heart who revels in the idea of being swept up in blissful love feeling.

The overall energy of the planet is cold, dangerous, erratic, and hostile. The darkness of ego in humankind has created an unsatisfactory turbulent life for so many that it's simultaneously hardened the hearts of souls who were born awakened and receptive to love. Somewhere along the way of their developmental stages as a child, this love was stomped out by the cruel ego in others. This made many on the planet unreceptive to love while deeply longing for it.

Someone gives you that rare smile as they walk past you and you don't know how to receive it. You're shocked that there was one person out of over seven billion who chose to warm up slightly in your presence. Because you don't know how to receive it due to not being used to it, you walk past them realizing you never acknowledged them back. It was only after you continued walking that you realized you couldn't believe you didn't smile back, but instead glared at them angrily annoyed. That's not receptive or being open to love at all. Who can blame you when Earthly life has beat down on your soul to the point of becoming closed off. You place your happiness on other people to prop you up and love you up, but that's an impossible demand to place on a species that is incapable of giving that unconditional love every second. Even the most compassionate loving person would desire a day off to not have to spread love on you. Only God and higher spirit beings are built to shower that undying, unwavering, and unconditional love on another full time every second of every moment of existence.

Every soul is born completely in tune, stress free, and filled with overflowing feelings of love, joy, and peace. As you coast through an Earthly life you come face to face with hostility, sometimes as early on as childhood while on Earth's elementary school playground. Most of this hostility is executed by another human soul through the darkness of their ego. It might be someone jaded and cut off from Spirit and God. You seek to find that one person on the planet that can give you that unconditional undying love that you crave only to be disappointed in the end.

When you have a mutual love with another person regardless of their gender, only then do you understand what God's love can feel like. This essence of God's love breathes life into your soul. It awakens and lifts you up to the most incredible euphoric high that is better than any drug or addiction. In fact, many who have been addicted to alcohol, drugs, food, or any other toxic vice have proclaimed to have lost interest in those addictions while in the throes of a beautiful mutual romance with someone else. This is partially because they're receiving the Dopamine chemical rush through true love feelings, which can be an addiction in itself, but it is less harmful than putting toxic substances into your body.

It's easy to grow lost and addicted to love. As a love addict, I know and understand all of the pitfalls and challenges that come along with that desire for love that never seems to reveal itself. Spirit understands this desire and craving human souls have for companionship with at least one person. This is a reciprocated companionship where the positive feelings for one another are mutual, rather than an unrequited love that can only cause heartache. This is one of the reasons that soul mates are put in your path. Spirit understands the desire that human beings have for a close companion and confidante. Even better is when that companionship is also passionate like in those romantic novels.

The human soul is not intended to endure a solo life even though most do or will end up doing into older age. This is why there are soul mates you cross paths with over the course of your journey to offer companionship and vice versa. You have more than one soul mate as all souls do. You ride up in an elevator with someone who strikes up a conversation with you. They end up saying something to you that has a positive impact. It could be a statement that changes your life. It gets you thinking, or it is an answer to an issue you needed solved. This is someone that was a soul mate in passing.

Soul mates come into your life for the purpose of your soul's growth. This might be done through teaching or offering you life tools that become helpful for you at a later date. A soul mate is the listening ear of someone you feel comfortable enough to talk to about a life issue. They help you through rough times where it would have been more difficult to get through had they not been there. I've certainly had more people than I can count tell me, "I honestly don't know how I could've got through that time in my life if it weren't for you. You were there for me day in and day out in ways that no one else was."

Soul mates are not all blissfully and unrealistically perfect. They challenge you and prompt you to look at the darker aspects of yourself that you would prefer to keep hidden. The soul mate helps to bring that out in order to help you improve, grow, change, and evolve. They do not bring these things out in an argument or out of cruelty. It is done out of love and with compassion because they care about you.

Potential soul mates cross paths with you for a variety of reasons. Most of them are with the intention of offering mutual soul lessons and growth. Some soul mates are intended to test you, coax you on, support you, and challenge you. Some of them might be to offer reminder blessings upon you such as in the form of positive optimistic words that help you to achieve something of importance, whether it's in the areas of work, spiritual, or personal life. Sometimes it can be to gain emotional traits that you didn't have before you met that person.

The purpose of other soul mate relationships is to offer you that mutual companionship that helps strengthen and support you along your Earthly journey. Some souls accomplish more while in a loving connection with another person. This helping you is a reciprocated one where you both learn and gain knowledge from one another that neither had before. Sometimes the soul mates goal is simply to remind you how to love. They are the catalyst that prompts you to change from being closed off and into a soul being that is open and receptive to love. Love is what keeps the Earth soaring around in the Universe and there isn't enough of it going around.

If you look back on all of the people you had connections with, you'll note some of the lessons learned while with them. There is always a lesson learned even if you don't believe there is or are unable to detect what that could be. If you don't know what the lesson is or was with a particular soul mate, then you'll be consistently met with the same situations being repeated and set up over and over again until you do. This is why some people have stated, "Why do I keep attracting in the same types of people into my life?"

Because the same lesson those mates are offering have not been fully realized and learned from by you. There is no time limit for learning lessons that contribute to soul growth. One specific lesson can take a week while another will take your entire Earthly life.

Other soul mate pairings grow to be doubly challenging where they show up in the form of a karmic relationship, as mentioned in the previous chapter. Karmic relationships tend to be bathed in antagonistic ego more than soul mate partnerships. They're usually unhealthy addictive connections that both partners cannot seem to stay away from. While at the same time there are still lessons and growth involved in those types of connections as well too.

Soul mates tend to challenge you and get you to notice things from a different perspective. This isn't to be confused with someone who is heartless or abusive. Abusive tempestuous connections formed with others are karmic relationships, even though not all karmic connections are abusive. This is where there is unfinished business that needs to be wrapped up with that soul. You'll continue to incarnate together until you gain wisdom from it or gain strength to eradicate the connection.

There are cases where both people in the karmic relationship gain and learn from it, while both evolve out of that and into a healthy positive soul mate connection with each other within the same lifetime. The connection dynamic shifts halfway through. Many couples that have lasted a lifetime together may appear at peace and contentment with one another in older age, but they may admit that it wasn't easy in the beginning. This could be because they started out as a karmic relationship that eventually graduated into a soul mate relationship.

CHAPTER SIX

Twin Flame Soul Connections

We've looked at karmic relationships and soul mate connections. The final spirit soul type of union is the twin flame. In Heaven, the twin flames are actually called twin souls, because they are souls that were made as one, but split into two. A great deal of people around the world can accept the idea of soul mates existing, but may not necessarily buy or believe in twin flames. Still we're going to look at them anyway since it's the third type of soul connection that can exist on Earth.

God does not have hard and fast rules jotted down on stone like the Ten Commandments when it comes to twin flames. What is discussed here about the twin flames is a generality of what most twin flame connections are like. You may see that you and your partner or potential friend of interest may fit some of the traits, but not all of them. This is about the personality traits fitting into most of the general guidelines my team has given me, but not necessarily every single one. It's to give you an overall idea of the nature of twin flames and how they are slightly different than the soul mates and karmic relationships you have throughout the course of your life. The twin flame is the highest form of a soul mate, which means the lessons they teach is enormous. You have numerous soul mates you cross path with, but only one twin flame.

There is quite a bit of contradicting information surrounding what a twin flame is, which has simultaneously caused all sorts of confusion. The reason it's caused misunderstanding is because when many talk about the twin flames today, they are discussing the feelings and emotions one feels when they meet their twin flame for the first time. The reason this causes misperception is because those intense feelings and descriptions are vague enough that they can be attributed to every single love relationship someone has ever had over the course of their entire life. Those feelings tend to exist for most anyone that has fallen in love or developed a love crush on another person. What makes the twin flame connection different than a love affair is the additional revealing stand out signs beyond the intense feelings one has. It is true the feelings for a twin flame are often intense, but that doesn't necessarily equate to a romantic union.

The feelings currently described for a twin flame are the same feelings used to describe when someone comes into contact with their soul mate or karmic relationship. Once that soul mate trend kicked in and grew to popularity, people started pining and longing for that one special love soul mate to come into their life and sweep them off their feet. Hollywood films then began to perpetuate the notion of finding your lifelong marriage love affair soul mate partnership through silver-screen stories. Romantic comedies in general have made billions of dollars displaying those stories on the big screen. They've made an enormous amount of money for the studios, production companies, and stars, because most everyone longs for that special love just like in the movies. They crave that one person they can live and mate with until death do you both part. The soul longs for the transcending kind of love that lifts them up into the clouds. Even the coldest person wouldn't necessarily shun some kind of positive attention from another person, since positive attention can be seen as love.

Everyone has more than one soul mate, which is becoming a bit more understood than it was pre-2015. It hasn't fully taken global understanding and effect yet. There are still people out there that are unaware they have more than one soul mate. These might be people who haven't necessarily studied up on it or connected with God for answers on it. Others don't believe in it or care much about it, but they have heard of the word phrase floating around.

The most jaded non-spiritual person may admit to saying the following statement upon meeting someone they deeply and intensely gravitate towards: "I think this guy/girl is my soul mate."

In the spiritual communities, the concept of understanding that you have more than one soul mate has become accepted and understood as the years progressed since my earlier books on soul mates and twin flames came out. This is mostly due to how easily information is now shared across the Internet. The negative side effect to that is false information can grow like wildfire on the Internet leaving masses of people to believe in something that isn't true. There is quite a bit of enormous confusion that starts to also rise as a result of that.

As people began understanding the spiritual truth that all souls have more than one soul mate sifting in and out of their life, then it became, "Well, that simply won't do. That takes away from the specialness of me being in love with that one special person for life that needs an appropriate label."

They then took the meaning of soul mates and transferred it over to be about twin flames instead. This is the same way man specifically altered the Bible in places in the later additions to fit a new narrative of life at that time, which would include all of the superstitions believed during that century.

Many have begun to understand that there is more than one soul mate, but only one twin flame. Since there is one twin flame, the thought has become, "Ahhh, well that sounds more distinct and I want something special."

They moved the feelings for the soul mate and transferred them over to mean about the twin flame. That notion has been lifted up and trended massively by those who are great at social media and getting their blogs noticed and picked up by websites. Now the latest growing trend is everyone is searching for that one special twin flame to fall in love and marry for life, except there are several issues with that. One of them being that your twin flame may not be a romantic partner nor will they be living on Earth at the same time you are.

Your twin flame is like a karmic or soul mate connection where it can be a friendship, family member, business partner, or lover. The reason twin flames don't necessarily incarnate at the same time as you is because you spend eternity with them back home on the Other Side. If you're spending an eternity with someone, but you embark on a separate soul mission to incarnate on Earth, then why would your twin flame follow you? There are rare circumstances where a twin flame will incarnate relatively in the same lifetime.

The latest trend has taken the truths about twin flames and swept all of those big hearts longing for love into a frenzy causing all sorts of confusion in the process. Everyone is now looking for that one twin flame to complete them the way Tom Cruise protested it to Renee Zellweger's character in the film *Jerry Maguire.*

Except in spiritual truth a soul is already complete before the twin flame merges with their split apart. Your soul is in a place of feeling complete and whole with a raising consciousness beyond the superficiality of the physical life before the twin flame shows up if they are going to show up at all.

This is why for so many people if the merging is going to take place in their lifetime, it typically happens later in life after a great deal of maturity, unless there is a large age difference, but even in those cases the younger duo of the partner has exceptional maturity for their age.

Twin soul flames are not always romantic in nature, as much as some would love to believe that the pretty imagery in some twin flame drawings and photos matches the romance novel kind of love found in those books. There are millions of people in the world that will never have a romantic partner. Many of them have accepted that. There are different reasons for why that is and many of them know and understand this reality. To have others shove an unrealistic truth and belief that every person on the planet will meet their romantic twin flame in their lifetime creates a deceptive dangerous situation for the receiver. To believe that everyone has a romantic partner waiting to unite with them is a delusional myth. Every person on the planet deserves love, but that doesn't mean that will realistically come about in the form of a love partner. It's mistaken to assume that everyone will meet someone in a passionate love making romantic relationship like in the movies, as wonderful as that idyllic dream might sound.

Like soul mates, your twin flame can be a different gender or sexual orientation than you, which would make the love relationship bit impossible and unrealistic to take place. It won't however change the binding feelings you have for one another because the twin flames are indefinitely inseparable in spirit. This is beyond any physical attraction.

This isn't to say that twin flames cannot be sexually and physically attracted to one another, but that's the least of their interests because the connection they have is a soulful one with a higher life purpose. It is their souls that are drawn to one another beyond the appearance. They can sense something strong within one another that pulls them towards each other. They feel as if they are looking in a mirror at themselves from a soul sense.

Having a mutual sexual physical attraction for someone is called lust. Lust for another person blinds you to the red flag warnings about someone else deceiving you into thinking you're in love with someone you just met. When you fall in love with someone you've just met, then it's more often than not a lust attraction first. This is why lust filled attraction relationships also tend to start up with this great passionate intensity before ending sooner than later. When it ends sooner than later, then that can indicate it was a lust filled physical attraction that had taken place and not a deep love. A deep love never wanes, dissolves, or goes away even if the two part indefinitely. It also endures throughout the years without ever faltering. A physical attraction can be deceiving into making you believe you're with the one only to discover the other person was never truly all that into you. Physical attraction can fade to some degree, whereas true deep love rarely fades.

The long running person you have more in common with on all levels minus the physical sexual attraction is more likely to be the twin flame over the person you have a lust filled sexual passionate physical attraction for. If twin flames coming together in their lifetime is due to assisting one another in a mission or purpose, then receiving that kind of support from someone you enjoy going to bed with to make love to because you find them hot, sexy, handsome, or cute is unlikely to be able to fulfill the demanding purpose of the twin flame.

Twin flames come together when they are rapidly evolving beyond the fads and trends of current modern-day society. Current modern functioning resides on the surface, but spiritual growth is higher up beyond the physical surface. The twin flames tend to be old souls regardless of their physical age due to the many lifetimes they've endured.

As a soul incarnates enough times, they grow to be more intelligent with a higher consciousness. God needs those souls to send on missions back to Earth to help usher in change as leaders, warriors, love showers, and teachers. That may not end up being the case as much as you or I might not want to come back while insisting this is it. Your perspective as a soul back home is much broader than it is on Earth. You take the mission of coming to Earth seriously before you incarnate again. In one sense, it is almost as if you are going off to fight a war or head to battle, because you know that is what it will feel like by agreeing to an

Earthly life. You will be navigating a battleground on a rock consumed and dangerously susceptible to being attacked by the dark energies.

If a twin flame connection is going to happen for someone, then the union doesn't necessarily happen right away. While their mutual private draw to one another may be silently explosive, they move and come together at a slower pace than other relationships. This is partially because evolved souls understand there is no rush when it comes to a serious connection. Other less disciplined souls will rush passionately into a hot romantic interlude that quickly fizzles sooner than one or both may have preferred. Twin flames are in a place of deep spiritual maturity before they come together. They will never rush into something overnight, nor will they push to make a connection happen as fast as possible. They move methodically and at a slower pace. With spiritual maturity and a raised consciousness, one has also grown more patient about certain things including life circumstances and coming together with someone.

If twin flame souls incarnate relatively around the same time, then they do this within the span of eighty years. This means they can show up when you're eight or when you're eighty. There tends to be a generational gap or age difference of about ten years or more give or take between twin flames. If it's a love relationship with a wider age gap, then this is sometimes a source of conflict in this ego-based world. The conflict is not necessarily between the twin flames who are equally evolved regardless of their age, but the conflict may come from outside influences that have placed a stigma on any kind of age gap, which is called ageism.

Most of the time there is an age gap that is largely considered to be against what some cultures or parts of society believe in, especially in the United States over any other country. The gap can extend extremely wide into decades, which would make it even more unlikely that the two will form a love relationship, but a deep friendship instead.

Another newer theory perpetuated is to believe the twin flame is primarily a physical sexual love connection. This was spread by those that fell for those artistic memes and images posted by others that show a man and a woman intertwined with the phrase *twin flames* above it. This is despite its offensiveness to some by using a man and a woman as the depiction image of a true authentic deep romance. Twin flames can be the same gender and are not always romantic. This information can be easily retrieved through any higher Divine related psychic communication.

There may be the obvious initial challenges between twin flames such as age related, gender, cultural, and so on. They may even be confused by the connection if it's moving into love relationship territory, because they've never felt that intensely for anyone before. Both partners experience this intense draw that never wavers.

Your twin flame can be of a gender that you're not attracted to. It's not necessarily a deep love relationship, but it is a deep love and adoration between those two people without the sexual component. It can be a parent-sibling connection, it can be lifelong business partners, and it can be siblings or best friends. It doesn't matter if someone is your twin flame or not because no one is going to get a special medal for re-uniting with their twin flame. Are you happy with someone and they're happy with you? Any healthy positive loving connection between two people regardless of their gender or label is what is important above anything else. It is the love that God and the angels adore seeing on a planet that is generally devoid of love.

A soul may choose to incarnate as gay or homosexual at any particular time in history. Some say it's not a choice, but the soul did choose to incarnate as homosexual in their soul's contract for various purposes knowing of the challenges that will arise in that role with current society, which still views gays through a primitive archaic lens. The soul may also have chosen to incarnate as straight or bisexual, but at around a certain age in their human life they'll change their sexual orientation. The media has shown the polar opposites of humankind not evolved enough to accept that all people are equal and deserve love. The ego would rather see homosexuals harmed or executed, which is not someone evolved or of God. Those that believe the twin flame connection is between a man and a woman in a romantic love relationship have no understanding of what a twin flame soul connection is, nor do they have any authentic connection with God, because when you do have that strong Divine connection, then the truth is in plain sight. It's all about soul love regardless of your outdated human belief value systems.

More people than not used to have hatred towards anyone who had a same sex attraction. Once they realized that every other person they loved around them fit that description, they gradually changed their tune realizing they made a mistake about their hatred, and just didn't know any better. Now it's becoming increasingly common, loved, and accepted, but there are still those living in the stone ages with a limited view that have yet to gain love for those not like them. They believe that the planet is normalizing same sex gay love, as if love between two people isn't normal. Sounds ironic considering that the reason all are here is to learn to love. You would think those that hold the biblical book so close to their chest could've gained that small amount of wisdom from it. Using Biblical text that was added in at a later date by superstitious fearful men isn't a good excuse, since God created all breathing life this way for a reason. God doesn't have hang ups about two souls in love with each other regardless of their gender. Love is what He desires to see, so in that instant when two souls are in love, He is pleased. In fact, God has disdain for those that express hatred over two souls in a committed love relationship. Jesus Christ was the same way. His complaint was over adultery and not about committed love between two souls. There are also non-believers that have hatred for gays, but the media gives the religious the hate card. Prejudices exist within all groups that exist on the planet.

When you're not evolving, then the potential

possibility of connecting with your twin flame is non-existent. It is the evolving souls that unite and merge with a twin flame partner for the purposes and goals of moving up to the next soul plateau beyond the physical realm.

One of the goals of all souls is to learn to accept all people in love. It is to learn to love and to give love. You learn that when you are thrown together with people who are not like you. You're not going to necessarily learn much by hanging around people that are your tribe and clan. People mark themselves off and stick to their own kind thus staying exactly where they are in their soul's growth process. It's human nature to behave in this primal instinctive way. It goes back to grade school when those who are like each other hang around one another in their little cliques and packs the way animals do.

When your twin flame is on the Other Side in the spirit world, they may work as one of your guides to bring soul mate connections into your life. They don't want you spending your days longing for love and companionship, so they assist in the process of bringing you potential lovers, friendships, colleagues, or acquaintances for soul mate connections.

Not everyone will experience a romantic love partnership, let alone one that lasts until the end of their days. This leads to the myth that there is someone out there for everyone, which is a misguided romantic notion that doesn't ring true for every single person on the planet. It's also a fictitious impractical assumption to feed the masses with. There are millions of people that will never obtain a love partner, or they may not be looking for one.

The twin flame is the ultimate deep love that transcends all. One of the common reasons all souls incarnate into an Earthly life is for the purpose of teaching and learning. The twin flames are together on the Other Side for all eternity, so there is little reason for both of them to incarnate into an Earthly life as well too, unless there is a larger reason, purpose, goal, and mission to do so. This would be one that requires the both of your Divine powers. The purpose of re-uniting on Earth isn't to be in a love relationship. There has to be something else that both are doing that points to their soul evolvement process.

The twin flame connections are not always love related, which on the one hand may be a blessing for some people. This is because if the two incarnate relatively at the same time during one lifetime and fall in love, then it will be more intense than if your twin flame was a best buddy or a business partner you've joined forces with for life.

Those around that witness a twin flame connection when they are together will point out the natural ease they notice both have as if they are made for each other. They will point out that they have the same essence, movements, and moods to one degree or another. And others may point out that they seem like they even look the same, even if they are physically different in appearance. There is something about the cosmic kismet like feeling that shows them to be two peas in a pod. Once together on Earth they never leave one another's side even if they break apart. The break might seem permanent, but more often than not it ends up being temporary. They wind back around to each other at a later date as if the break never happened. This is due to the strong running soul pull between the both of them that never seems to leave even while physically apart.

The twin flame connection intensity is not necessarily a fun feeling to be in. It's uncomfortable and confusing for both people at times that sometimes it feels easier to just leave or keep their distance, so they don't drown in its intensity. That is until both are mature enough to ease into this intensity so that it works for all parties involved.

There are rare cases where the twin flames never unite back into a romantic relationship due to the self-sabotage or disruption that one of the partners executes, but they will never truly disappear. Instead they will forever pop up from time to time with a text, email, or phone call throughout the duration of both of your lives. You'll both wonder why it never transformed into something more again if it doesn't seem to. The exceptions are if the twin flames are not lovers, but friends or relatives, or if the age gap is so wide where one is twenty and the other is seventy years old. The deep connection love is always present even if it's not romantic due to a variety of human physical factors. It is rare for a twin flame soul connection to break apart in any other duo except love. Love relationships are always more challenging than any other connection in general, so it's no surprise that this is doubly so in a twin flame connection.

There isn't necessarily an order of how any of these types of relationships come about. Those who are in one dysfunctional relationship after another are typically encountering karmic connections. Some people will have several long-term love relationships that were soul mate connections, but ones that didn't go the distance. If a twin flame connection is to come about, then it will at some point later into adulthood after other relationships have been experienced first.

There are a great many people who meet someone in High School and get married and remain with that person for the duration of both their lives with little to no karmic issues. These are the general soul mate relationships. There are people that never have the luxury of being in any kind of long-term love relationship, some by choice and others because it just never happens for them.

This higher mission is not about coming together in humankind's holy matrimony, even if the twin flames are romantic in nature. There must be a higher mission beyond coming together that transcends a human relationship. This longing you have for your twin flame is a longing for love to fill the aloneness you might sometimes feel. This can be remedied with a stronger connection with God, Divine and Spirit. It can be relieved through the various potential companions God places in your path.

More often than not, one's twin flame is on the Other Side working with you to bring in soul mate relationships. They are in charge of the love relationships you have throughout your life because they know it contributes to your soul's growth. They will sometimes also work with your own guides on helping you fulfill your purpose.

Like God and your Spirit team, you can call on your twin flame if they are on the Other Side for assistance in the areas of love, but also when it comes to your mission. They are more than happy to come in and help because they are a part of you, and you are a part of them. They know when they are helping you that they are simultaneously helping their own evolvement process.

If they are on Earth during your lifetime, then you'll find that there is an eerie kind of mirror action going on with your twin flame. It is like a push and pull running and chasing situation happening. This doesn't go on indefinitely. It can go on as long as it needs to before you two come together. This means it might take one month or it might take many years. There is no set timeline especially with twin flames. Because the connection is felt deeply on an intense level it can go on for a bit before the union has lift off. This is regardless if it's a friendship or potential love relationship. The deep intensity is across the board regardless of the physical nature of the union.

If you travel to centuries past and you got married to someone, but then met your twin flame it would've caused confusion and torment. This is especially due to the time period frowning on divorce. If you got married to someone and met your twin flame back in history, then you ended up having to either let them go or have a discreet affair that ended up causing all sorts of Earthly controversy. It was frowned upon if a man had a deep love for another man and a woman had a deep love for another woman. This is still frowned upon by half the world, but the other half of the world has been awakened enough to fully understand that it is God's will that souls learn about love in ways beyond their primal archaic mind can fathom.

There is a serenity feeling for both partners in a twin flame connection, but that's not always experienced right away. When they first run into each other, they have an immediate curiosity with one another needing to know who that person is. Their mutual eye contact says it all. This part is like the movies in the beginning where they see each other from across the room. They might be talking to someone else, but find themselves constantly looking over with a smile or dancing eyes, and you're doing the same thing. It isn't so much the physical attraction, but a cosmic soul attraction. Both partners feel this exceptionally strong pull they've never felt before in that way with anyone to that degree. It's unexplainable for the both of them and they mutually want to get closer. This is regardless if the person becomes a love relationship, friendship, or any other dynamic. The intensity for both is the same.

The twin flame connections have a push and pull situation going on at first, but this isn't to be confused with co-dependency. Co-dependency exists primarily in karmic relationships. With twin flames it is that the feelings for one another are too intense for the both of them. Neither partner is used to feeling a love that deeply with someone else before. This pushes the ego reaction to shun it, hesitate, or move super slow in coming together. The feelings are too overwhelming in ways that neither felt before. This brings on a certain excitement enveloped with fear as well too.

When twin flames come across one another for the first time they both immediately notice that there is something different about the other one that feels awfully familiar on a soul level. Even if it's not an immediate romantic love feeling, there is something emotionally strong and unexplainable, because as previously stated twin flames are not always love relationships, even though there is a great deal of love and respect moving between them. It's beyond the physical and the first thing they both notice is the telepathic emotional sense picked up on, rather than the guy or girl is hot, since the latter is typically a lust filled physical carnal attraction and connection. The attraction between twin flames is beyond a physical attraction, even if that part of the equation is present. It is primarily a soul attraction above anything else.

CHAPTER SEVEN

Benefits and Challenges of Technology Dating

There can be nothing greater than in-person soul connections uniting in the physical world. This is where you can go to the movies with someone, go to dinner together, talk face-to-face with them, or kiss and hug a mate. In-person connections build a deeper soul history filled with profound memorable nostalgic experiences. When you spend the day at an amusement park or a nature retreat with a lover or a friend, then more often than not you find you've grown closer and more connected with each other by the end of the trip. This is because you were building a deeper in-person connection and having a three-dimensional experience.

Deeper chemistry is created when you're hanging out with someone physically in a space together. This has grown more challenging to do with the rise of technology. The benefits to technology are how easy it can be to connect with most anyone. The negatives are that people often complain that it either doesn't move into an in-person connection or doesn't measure up to what they thought it would be in-person. Technology gives one an illusion of who people think you are only to be stunned at how dramatically different the person ends up being in-person.

I started out in the film industry working, conversing, and being friends with hundreds of well-known talents. This was throughout the 1990's and into the 2000's before social media became a thing. Whenever I would meet one of them for the first time, they were always much more dramatically different in appearance and personality in-person than the images of them on screen, in the media, in the news or in magazines. It was like sitting with anybody else, except they looked familiar, but on a smaller level. By the time the Internet took off with social media and dating apps, I was already versed in this interesting phenomenon of how dramatically different someone is in-person. But now the rest of the world was becoming privy to this notion through the use of the Internet, social media, and dating apps. You are building someone up online who you think is one way only to find that they are much different in-person. The real clue as to if it is a connection that will go the distance is when you spend numerous times in-person.

Sending a text, chat words, or email comes off distant and transactional. It dehumanizes others where you end up treating them as if they're a robot without feelings or emotions. This is why it's so easy for others to ghost, block, or ignore you online or on an app. You're no longer a living breathing soul in that person's eyes. You're just a picture with a name on it is all. They're not necessarily doing this with malice. They don't realize the deeper consequence to their behavior that's being tallied up in your soul contract as to how you may or may not be dismissing others. This has added to an entirely new set of lessons for soul growth being applied to humankind.

Ghosting is when you're dating someone, and then you end the connection by disappearing without a trace. No warning, no words, and nowhere to be found. This isn't to be confused with someone you have no interest in engaging with and nor is it saying to force an engagement when you're not feeling it. This is more of a generalization as to how the behavior is overall. It's easy to dismiss, drop, and eradicate someone via technological means. I had an ex break up with me twice via impersonal means. The first time was through an email message on the social media site My Space when that site was the #1 social media site over all others. The second time this ex broke up with me was years later via a handwritten note left on my door. As you may or may not have likely guessed, this particular ex was obviously around for many years leaving me in this same way, but never truly leaving.

There are a great number of people that are left in similar ways never to hear from the person again. It's easier for someone to leave people today through the impersonal technological ways. You lose the risk of in-person confrontation or having to deal with how the other person might react knowing that it might not be good. If it's someone that once meant the world to you one might think the diplomatic choice would be to at least talk to them in-person. That's how it used to be done before the days of technology. Some call it the cowardly way out or being disrespectful, but some do it to avoid confrontation. This doesn't make it okay, but it is the world we live now.

With technology you're treated like a no name suspect even if they know you. You're just a digital name on the screen at that point. As a result, the emotional factor underneath an email or a text on a screen can be misinterpreted. This is also why it's never wise to have serious discussions via text or email. It is also why many people have complained about being discarded by potential friends or lovers they've connected with online by being ghosted. If they're lucky, then they might receive an email, letter, or text. Sometimes there is no explanation, but the person gradually distances themselves and shows less interest in the person. When this happens, then some will take it harder than others to have their ego bruised in what they deem to be a hurtful way.

There are common behaviors that have become more acceptable etiquette even if it bothers some people. For example, if it's someone you were chatting with online or on a dating app for a few weeks and they suddenly drop the ball and move on, then you move on. Developing intense love feelings over someone you've never met and have only been chatting with a short amount of time can lead to a dangerous outcome. The person that drops the ball in the chatting is also chatting with many others at the same time. They don't owe you anything if you haven't met in person and have gone on at least a number of dates. It's become acceptable behavior in the dating app sphere to drop the ball in communication for good if you don't actually know each other.

This also goes for business relationships. Because so much business is done online you may find that your sole connection with colleagues or clients is through email, phone, or a chat program. This diminishes the quality of the connection into something colder and distant. Imagine the entire planet communicating this way and you can see how that has hardened and chilled the world to love. Love has a challenging time penetrating the technological sphere.

Technological connections have a remote distance to them because you are controlling what you're putting out there into the world. You decide what to type to another person in a text, an email, in a comment box, or on a social media post. This gives the illusion of having a deeper connection that may be one-sided. You're not absorbing the three-dimensional aspects that make up a person when you're in the same room with them.

Another reason it is growing increasingly rare is due to the domination of the darkness of ego. Many lack follow through with the endless choices at their fingertips. It is easy to discard others when you have a technological device. There have been numerous studies indicating that people don't know what to do when they have too many choices. Having a few choices is one thing, but you're twenty-seven and you have 1,600 matches on your Tinder dating app, but no love relationship and no prospects.

Some think if they swipe yes/right on as many people they initially find attractive that one of those thousands of matches is bound to be a match, yet this isn't necessarily the case. I've dove into the dating school of hard knocks to try it both ways. The first was to collect as many matches as possible to see if that works. Thousands of matches later, I was overwhelmed at the number of messages pouring in. I couldn't keep up and grew stressed out over it because I'm someone that likes to get back to people in general. When you have dozens of people messaging you at the same time each day, then it can quickly become overwhelming. One of the other issues I was faced with was the shotgun way that matches were attempting to go about it. They would message me with the initial *how-are-you's*, and then I'd message back with the same. They'd come back with, "Would you be interested in meeting up?"

I'd yank my head back…umm, no. I just said six

words to you. From those six words you already want to meet up? This tells me you're basing your interest on me due to your physical lust filled attraction. That does not automatically equate to in-person chemistry in other areas. Communication style, values, and interests are what bond people together. If you're incapable of communicating with the person you're communicating with on a dating site or app, then how are you going to transfer that to in-person success?

The shotgun method potentials were physically attracted to me, so in their eyes they wanted to nail me so to speak. This isn't just one person immediately asking to meet up in this way. There were dozens coming in at the same time on a regular basis. I thought if I dropped everything to meet up with every single person that was saying hello to me and asking to immediately meet up, then I'd never get anything done. For the purpose of research, I did try out the method of agreeing to meet those shotgun people to see if maybe it could work. Unfortunately, I found that meeting that way ended up being a waste of time. When you don't take the time to get to know someone first with some communication banter, then you are unable to detect if it's someone you'd have a good camaraderie with.

When you are engaging in banter with someone on an app or online before meeting it's not always to waste time without ever meeting. It's to see if you have anything in common and a flowing rapport before meeting in-person. If you're both incapable of online app banter, then the likelihood of carrying that into an in-person meeting will be high. It will be unlikely that either of you will have much to say and there's nothing worse than sitting there struggling to say something that would be of interest to either of you. Meeting the shotgun way typically ends up being disastrous. Whereas the ones that engaged in app banter because they genuinely enjoyed communicating to you and getting to know you ended up translating successfully in-person.

The other extreme are those that chat for months and months, but have shown no interest in meeting. When you've brought up getting together at some point, then that was shut down, brushed aside, or excuses were made. This is a sign they are currently just interested in online communication banter. Some do this out of boredom, others delay meeting due to a shyness and uncertainty about the connection, while others do it because they're hiding something. If they do show interest and admit to wanting to get together at some point, then they've shown interest in taking it to another level….one day. There are also the busy professionals. If you want someone that is independent and has their own life, then you expect that the person will be busy often, which tends to be the case with professional achievers. It's either that or go after someone who has nothing going on in their life. Every time you message them, they quickly message back because they are never doing anything, which is the other extreme.

If you're in a rush to seal the deal with anybody,

then continue chatting and dating around keeping your options open. You should be doing that anyway until you've landed on someone that piques your interest as much as you do with them.

I've also tested out the dating apps where I would only match with a select small group of people. This is by keeping the match list under twenty instead of into the thousands. I would then focus on developing a connection with each of them to see how conversational style is on the dating app. If they are giving one to three-word phrases, then they're showing they don't have enough energy to muster to communicate with someone properly. This will carry over to the in-person meeting, which would be a waste of time. The same goes for those that drop the ball in the online app banter which shows they've grown bored, distracted, or moved onto someone else on the app as does tend to be the case, so don't take that personally.

I would also give people time to respond before unmatching them. The date of the last communication is on there so I would look to see if it's been over a month since our last communication before unmatching them. Some people unmatch way too soon if they don't get a response within a day or two, which is unreasonable and unrealistic in today's world. I'm being super generous by giving them a month. People get busy, lives become a distraction, others get consumed over matters not realizing time has passed. Someone is not going to make a stranger a priority. I've also had people come back to me weeks later after they were going through something, then we just pick up where we left off. Many of those people ended up becoming friends or great dates, because they also weren't under the pressure of giving someone twenty-four hours exactly to get back to them, otherwise you've blown it. I've also met those that are that strict unable to accept that it may take some people time to get back to them. Those same people have also been single and living on these apps indefinitely. It hasn't sunk in that this rapid-fire way of demanding one keep messaging you is not working. That's not an inviting warm person that many would feel comfortable knowing or getting to know. I've had more success with having a smaller match list over having a larger match list. You put in more effort with people when you have a few to focus on rather than collecting matches for reasons that have no benefit at all.

The current dating app at this time that may have the edge is Bumble. Bumble keeps your match list clean to an extent. It works in the same way that Tinder and OK Cupid does. This is where you both have to swipe right on each other's profiles before you end up in one another's match list. Only when you're in each other's match list can you then message the person. I like this feature because you're not having random people hitting you up out of nowhere. If someone messages you, then you know you already matched with this person, which shows an element of interest present due to being matched.

Bumble takes it a step further where it gives you

a short amount of time to send a message to your new match. If neither of you send a message within about 24 hours, then you will both expire from the match list and eventually drop off the grid. This works since many have found the method of Tinder to not be as effective. Tinder keeps your matches in your list until the end of time or you delete them or your profile. It's pointless having a large match list if no one is messaging one another. There is no edge or advantage to that.

The negative about Bumble's method is the amount of time allotted to message a new match is super brief. It's not always enough time especially for a busy professional. The quality matches for a long-term relationship tend to be people that are independent and professionally driven. Someone that doesn't have those qualities leans towards the co-dependent. When someone has too much time on their hands, they will demand more of your time, or they will seek it out by continuing to chat with others who can satisfy their boredom and feed them the attention they crave.

Bumble also works on algorithm's where it shows you the matches they think are quality matches first. How do they determine what a quality match is? They base it on the profiles that get swiped right more than others. Of course, we know that the profiles that tend to get swiped right the most are the ones where the person appears physically attractive in some way to the user. This does not necessarily equate to long-term material and compatibility. It also further emphasizes the truth that people look at physical appearances first before even bothering to pay attention to that person.

These apps and this concept may be outdated if you're reading this at a later time in history, but there may be something comparable you can apply it to. If anything, you can know what was popular when I was around.

Trading long chats, texts, and emails with a potential friend or lover can help both parties get to know one another before meeting and connecting in person. The danger is if one places more emphasis and feeling on the fact that this person is sharing so much with them that they have a shot at developing something more serious. That is until you find out the person you've been sharing emails with had no deep interest in you and was merely an exceptional conversationalist via email. The other danger is you fill in the blanks of what you believe this person's motive is or isn't only to discover they're married or have no deep emotion for you. The positives to technological conversing with people you know is keeping in touch, especially if you don't physically live near one another.

In-person connections are rare since most people today remain in contact through the technological ways available. This has made others lazy in connecting in-person. There are other reasons that prevent in-person connections from happening that are valid such as you work a hard job professionally that demands a great deal of time from you. It's easy to connect with people via technology, text, email, or social media today, but more challenging to connect in-person. Why would someone connect in-person when they have so much to do and it's far easier to hop on a quick phone call with them?

Some have become pickier about what they desire in a love partner. There is nothing wrong with having high standards to an extent, but you also don't want to have them so high that you rule out potentials sent your way. I've come across men and women who have the long lists of what they do or do not want on their dating profiles. These are those super restricting stats of what they want in a potential person for a relationship. I've read profiles that might say, "No one under thirty." Or, "Your body and weight should be proportioned." Or, "I'll know what I like when I see it."

People really do put that and much more in their profiles, which in one sense is wise because then you know what you're getting if you choose to engage with someone like that. They will inevitably be negatively criticizing and critiquing how you look and what you say or do. I've also found those with the strict lists of what they want also end up unable to find anyone that fits the bill. They also live on the dating apps and sites indefinitely.

If something like someone's physical fit appearance is important to you, then the appropriate phrase should be something like: "I'm a physically active person and enjoy sports related activities. I'm looking for a partner in crime with similar interests in that arena to share that with."

At the same time, I've had people inform me that they'll have someone they matched with tell them they are interested in something like hiking in the way they are. But they discover this isn't true when they end up going on a legitimate hike only to find the person cannot hack it so to speak. This is because the other person that said they loved hiking was confused by what a genuine hike is. They assumed it was the kind of hike that posers see as a hike where you stroll in nature with a friend to chat. Serious hikers are hiking in rougher inclines in a nature setting that can last several hours and sometimes a good chunk of the day.

If deep down you know that you cannot handle anyone not fitting the bill of your picture-perfect ideal messaging you, then make that list for yourself, then file it away. Jot that down in an email or notepad for your eyes only. Don't put it in your profile, but make the list of the traits of the kind of person you'd like to be with in a relationship. Write that letter to God and your Spirit team, then email that to yourself and let it go. Allow what the Universe is intended to bring you to come to fruition.

You can have the secret mental list of what you desire, but when you let it go, you also let go of those restrictions. You keep an open mind in accepting the partner that is intended to match up with you, even if they don't match your statistical requirements. I've made those lists in the past and ended up with people that didn't necessarily fit the description, but we met and fell in love. When it comes to love in the end, those lists are discarded anyway. Ultimately, the one for you is not what you will be expecting. Many have admitted that their current life love partner was not someone they were typically attracted to or would have gone after, but now that they're with them they wouldn't have it any other way.

There are the more reasonable requests such as wanting to date a non-smoker, or if you're in Alcoholics Anonymous, then naturally you may not want to be in a potential relationship with someone that is a heavy drinker. There are the deal breakers that you know you cannot accept at all. Then there are the rules that you're relaxed about. These are rules that you know you could fold on and accept about someone in a relationship. If you won't fold on any of your rules, then you could end up single until the end of your life. You need some measure of compromise knowing that there is no perfect person that is interested in every single thing you are. Compromising is one of the bigger traits that are going to be required of anyone in any kind of connection.

Placing any kind of demand on others to give you the attention and love you crave will only end in disappointment. Souls are flawed and imperfect as people. They will disappoint especially when you are expecting them to be a certain way. When you want others to adapt to you, then you can be sure they will steer clear of you in the end. When you try to push someone to be your friend, then the more you push them away. No one will be your friend because you're demanding them to be your friend. Don't chase after people to give you what you crave. This is the same way you can't force someone to be in a relationship with you. When you push your mate for a stronger commitment with a list of demands when they're not in that space, then this turns them off causing them to eventually distance themselves from you. No one likes the idea of being caged or boxed in to do something out of force. The same goes for friendships or acquaintances. The successful connections that take place happen organically and naturally without force.

Nothing in the physical material world will fill up any emptiness in you. Certain aspects might temporarily fulfill someone for a brief spell, but it will not last longer than a day. The true measure of success is where your soul's growth is in moving through its personal transformation and evolution. Avoid getting caught up in the fantasy that is revealed to you through technology. Instead focus on your soul's personal journey by finding ways to awaken and open up your consciousness to the love that exists within the Light.

One of the positives of technology is that it has brought transparency to light in a manner that has never before been seen in history. In Heaven, no one can get away with a lie the way they can on Earth, but this is gradually shifting as everything is being pushed into the spotlight. The difference between Heaven and Earth in that respect is that beings in Heaven aren't dishonest in character. All spirit beings in Heaven are bathed in compassion, strength, and love full time. Whereas on Earth, a great many human beings are operating from the darker side of their nature.

The smaller percentage of the population that expresses compassion and understanding most of the time tends to be Earth Angels. They see the good and the best in others, but have great distaste or offense towards anyone that displays toxicity. Some of those personalities are Wise Ones that might be a younger appearing person who has exceptional poise that they come off as if they're hundreds of years old. This is because their soul is much older than their human years. They have chosen to incarnate on Earth for various purposes that include bringing much needed love to the planet.

There are good and bad elements to anything that was created. If two mature thinking evolved beings can find each other on an app and forge a lifelong committed relationship or best friendship, then this is the positive side to connecting on a technical app. When you find that great big rare love, then treat it like gold because it is a rarity. The two evolved souls that reside in the space of love will find one another regardless of the obstacles put in their path of the current modern-day human climate, which has been as tumultuous as it was centuries ago.

You have free will choice, which can negate and alter what is intended to take place. Your soul contract may reveal a particular love soul mate that will show up at a particular time in your life. Due to free will choice on your part and/or this other person's part, it can alter and change both your paths pushing the connection further out or from happening at all.

Sometimes the future soul mate love partner will show up while you're still in a love connection that was supposed to end. You feel a strong gravitational pull towards that new person even though you might not romantically act on anything with them. Both teams of guides from your side and this other person's side are aware that the old connection is going to end, so they jump the gun and orchestrate the bumping into part of this new person knowing nothing might take off for awhile.

For some people connections take time before having full lift off that it's safe enough to bring the newer soul mate in and let it take its time evolving into more down the line. Meanwhile, the former love connection has fulfilled its contract agreement and begins to disband. It isn't long before the new love interest begins to have lift off.

When two souls are ready and evolved enough, then the lifelong love partnership will happen when either expects it. You will both be placed on the same path where it is orchestrated perfectly to the point where you're both standing face to face. There is no way either of you cannot see it.

You might be afraid to approach your crush for fear of being rejected, but if it's someone you can't get your mind off of, then take the risk to at least say hello to this person. Gauge their interest level after saying hello and notice if they seem standoffish because they're not interested or unfriendly due to shyness. Some people have given up a potential love interest that is intended for them out of fear, or they'll avoid approaching a potential partner out of fear. Fear is one of the greatest causes of human sabotage holding people back.

CHAPTER EIGHT

Single and Longing for a Relationship

It's the human condition to feel bouts of loneliness or crave a passionate merging with a love partner. Being single for a prolonged period of time sucks for some people, while others have an easier time making the best of it and will live their daily life without that craving for a love relationship. The rest struggle to survive being alone.

If you can't change your relationship status tomorrow, then get with the program of the current dating market and protect yourself with the way it is now. Have a greater understanding of how the modern-day world of dating and relationships are at this point in Earth's history. Do your best to make the most of the state you're currently in. This is about making sounder decisions and learning to treat others with respect. This carries far into one's life where you can apply common sense etiquette to most anything.

You might be someone that loves being single and has no problem with it or you might desire a love partner. The longer it takes to obtain one, the more it feels as if you're trying to survive being single when you anxiously want to be in a relationship. You desperately wish you had a lover who loved you back with equal fervor, yet any and all potential prospects constantly evade you.

One of the ways of surviving modern day dating and relationships in a loveless world is by armoring yourself with knowledge. This includes knowledge over the way things currently are. You can read all of the love and relationship self-help books available on the market and still feel nowhere closer to obtaining a love relationship than you are now. You've went to psychic readers, you've cast spells, you put yourself out there, did the vision boards, the crystal meditations, and other love rituals presented to you, but you still find you're desperately wishing the person of your dreams was here already. You begin to grow more cynical as you grow older feeling as if it will never happen and that you just have to accept the fact that perhaps it's not in the cards.

You've grown permanently negative about not being able to attract in a love partner, so you debunk the tips that all of the love related self-help books have offered you. You're angry, frustrated, and over it. It's understandable that you've grown weary from battle in the love department, but this is not going to attract a stranger to you who could be the potential mate. You'll also stop bothering to put in an effort, as you've grown exhausted over the process. I don't blame you as I've been there too. I've had periods throughout my life where I've had to survive being single. When each of my past long-term love relationships ended, I would believe that was it. There would be no one else after that. As time progressed on and I seemed to be in a place of contentment, then a new soul mate would enter the picture. Rinse and repeat. It was anything but over for me.

Love is where all human souls are intended and expected to be, but most have strayed as far away from that space as possible. They've fallen victim to the mundane practical stresses of life, struggling to make a living, pay bills, buying groceries, and whatever it takes to survive in day-to-day functioning. Secretly somewhere deep down in that person's soul they long for some measure of a personal life that brings in a welcome relief and release in the form of a love partner. By the time you're done working you're too exhausted to sit face to face with another stranger, so you take the slim pickings that come to you seriously. You won't go out with just anyone who hits you up simply because they're attractive.

During my dating research moments, I've found that the some of the potentials that hit me up seemed to have too much time on their hands. They limit their messages to you in a series of one to three-word sound bite phrases while expecting to meet in ten minutes. This shotgun method of connecting with others doesn't work and nor does it bring you quality connections. For one, these are prospects that don't have anything going for them, which is why they have an abnormal amount of free time on their hands. Usually when someone wants to meet that quickly is because they only have one thing in mind and that is to ultimately get it on. This is one of the pitfalls to the dating app method of connecting. There is no way to filter out prospects by professionals or those with likeminded interests. You basically get everyone and their family hitting you up.

The love market has changed drastically as it seems to every ten years. The 1990's were the final decade where love and relationships would never be the same again. The technological age took off bringing the masses gained access to computers and cell phones, which later brought about dating websites, social media, and phone apps. There are definite pros to this as well as the cons to consider as there are to most anything. Having all of these fantastic choices around you sounds awesome initially, but humankind has a built-in ego, which causes one to wrestle with and vacillate between making decisions that work and ones that backfire. What came out of the technological age post 2000's is that it became easier to find sex than to find love. Love grew to be lacking more than it ever has in Earth's history.

There are more singles around the world than those in a relationship. Post 2000's was when the shift began to happen. The media, popular culture, and the high accessibility to technology heavily promoted sex instead of love at a rapid rate. The more a pop artist bumped and grinded on stage or in a video wearing little clothing, then the more popular they became. Popular culture was feeding and selling sex to the point where it was suddenly boring and unexciting.

After talking to and interviewing countless people, I discovered they all desired a long-term love relationship, but it was constantly evading them. It was difficult to understand, as they were independent, good looking, had a great personality, had their own money, we're caring, and compassionate. What was missing?

The main reason all exist is to LOVE. What else did you think you were here for? Is it to work a job? A job that will one day vanish once your run is complete? Jobs are a necessary means of physical survival, but it's not why you're here unless the job is connected to your life purpose. One doesn't need to be married to their job to the point where they have no personal life. Hopefully, you find meaningful work that is your passion, but that's not the sole reason you are here. In the end, it's all about love, yet that seems to be a major struggle to achieve for most. Wallowing in perpetual negativity, sadness, hate, bitterness, and deceit seems to be a much better space to live in. This must be the case since the energy saturating the primary masses around the world swim in the epicenter of its toxicity. Notice the continuing noise of the media and social media with all those negative words being darted at one another. This gives you a great clue as to where humanity is at in the love department.

While the challenges to finding love have increased, it's not impossible to find that one person for life who desires what you want with you. Attracting in a suitable romantic partner entails loving yourself like nobody's business and believing in all that you are. This is all part of the self-love we discussed earlier in the book. Confidence is one of the key traits that attracts in others to your light and overall essence and energy. This doesn't mean you won't be attracting all sorts of prospects from all avenues, even from those who are not looking for something serious. It includes those unwanted proposals that see you primarily as a piece of meat to help them get off. You have to weed out a great deal of people while on the hunt for love. The potential partner is the needle in the haystack and the diamond in the rough that stands out. The majority of prospects seem to only be interested in sex rather than forming a soul mate love connection with someone. You have to have faith and patience that this soul mate love is out there.

Giving up on love is understandable and certainly not uncommon. Many have protested they've hit a point where they announce that love might not be in the cards for them. They've reached a place where they accept that. It's been years and all they have witnessed is one loveless situation after another. I came across someone who had gone ten years without ever having dated, and then out of nowhere met someone they fell in love with and ended up getting married, so love can happen when you least expect it.

Everyone is having a difficult time where love relationships are concerned because you've got part of the world desiring a love relationship, are already in a relationship, or want to be free. The best freedom in the world is when you're in the right love connection with someone who understands you and supports you, while you give that to them in return. Live life for you with just enough room for another loving soul to merge in with you.

You have more people than ever operating from the selfish ego. There is no room for another person when you're in that space. You're expecting the most perfect love partner to enter the picture that bows down and caters to all of your needs. I often hear others tell me what they will only accept in a partnership. It's this long list of outlandish requests, which limits the possibility of inviting in the right person. It should be about what you have to offer someone else and not what they can give you.

Let's say that you are spending your days longing for a romantic partner. If your Spirit Guide and Guardian Angel are working with you on other day-to-day situations, then you may have another guide or angel who joins you in your life assisting you on your search for the kind of soul mate that would be beneficial for you. This Spirit will work with your soul mates Spirit team in order to bring you two together.

You could be a busy professional and not active in the dating world aside from joining dating sites and dating apps to get to know potential suitors. Or perhaps you have done that, and it resulted in disappointment. This assigned "love guide" works with this other potential's guides to help you two to connect. You find you suddenly start crossing paths with the same person repeatedly at the store, at the gym, in an elevator, or even in a parking garage. There is a reason behind running into this same person consistently out of the blue. You are attracted to them, and you notice they seem to be taking notice of you in a positive warm way, yet you both brush it off or do not act on it. This is partly due to your ego, fear, and partly how technology has trained others to communicate via technical devices, but rendered them incapable when face-to-face. Both of your Spirit team's will continue to work on getting you both together. Yet it is up to the both of you to do the rest of the work. This work includes something that might be difficult for some such as saying hello.

If you find that every time you run into this person the butterflies rise, you grow nervous, or feel inadequate, then mentally in prayer ask God and your Spirit team to help give you confidence and courage to communicate. What's the worst that is going to happen if you make a mistake by saying hello? The other person says nothing or reacts in a way that wasn't what you were expecting. At least you did it rather than spending your days, weeks, and months wondering what if.

It is difficult for two people coming together in this day and age where primary means of communicating to each other is through technological devices. Now you're standing in front of someone and you're suddenly a mute. This other person is likely just as nervous as you. They might be kicking themselves for not responding adequately. If you continue to run into this person, then you'll both grow more comfortable with the other one being around. It will get easier to begin conversation even if it's always a *hi, hello, how are you.*

There are no missed opportunities. If the soul mate you are intended to connect with is meant to happen, then it will. If it doesn't, then another soul mate will be brought to you to match where you are at on your soul's evolution.

Desiring a love partner should not be misconstrued to be co-dependent. The human soul desires the company of other human souls, even if it's just one person in a companionship setting. This is why many support groups consider solitary confinement to be inhumane. If you were deserted on an island, then no matter how much you love yourself you would start to go crazy after a while. This is despite those who are independent and prefer to be alone. I've come across quite a number of people that prefer a solitary life, but even they have those moments where they are surfacing and desiring some attention from another on occasion. To equate a basic human need with desperation is absurd.

Some people have stronger emotional endurance when it comes to being alone. There are also many people who do not cope well with loneliness. Some of them resort to suicide, while others resort to drugs, alcohol, or sexual promiscuity.

Studies have also indicated that infants who do not receive touch in orphanages have a higher mortality rate. The same goes for senior citizens in care homes. This evidence suggests that human souls need both friendships and camaraderie, not to mention love and intimacy companionship.

You find that you've been doing the work by focusing on hobbies you enjoy and self-improvement activities, but this still leaves you wondering if a love partnership will ever happen. Love circumstances happen when you least expect it. When you fixate harshly on it coming about, then it delays and frustrates the love from entering the picture. Attempting to rigorously find a love partner generally results in disappointment. I've had many serious long-term relationships and every single one of them came about naturally and without effort. They came about when I wasn't expecting it or looking for it. Each partner showed up out of nowhere and then the union was driven in full speed motion. It was almost as if they fell on my doorstep when I wasn't looking for a relationship. As cliché as it might sound, they were chance encounters where we turned the corner and bumped into one another physically, "Oh! Sorry. Are you alright?"

Dialogue happened and the communication sifted effortlessly and excitedly back and forth. Boom! The connection was made, and phone numbers were exchanged.

I wasn't actively looking for a love relationship or waiting for one when all of my past partners showed up in the form of a dating or a love relationship. We bumped into one another randomly or they discovered me through other avenues. Our communication began to build into something more over the course of many months.

I haven't run into any cases where someone was deliberately and desperately searching for a love relationship and then it came to them. At the same time putting in an effort is better than sitting on your couch waiting for your next soul mate to ring your doorbell. Love connections happen when you least expect them to. When you expect a love relationship to happen, then that prevents, delays, and blocks it from happening. It also creates frustration energy, which pushes it further away from you. Love can never be forced, but at the same time you put in a bit of effort while keeping your heart and mind open to all possibilities and prospects.

Incidentally, I've reviewed cases where those that were happy, single, and not interested in a love relationship were the ones that effortlessly ended up in a love relationship. When you let go of the need to be in a relationship, then the closer you are to being in one.

Some cultures still prefer on deciding within the family unit who they think you should marry, but this is imposing your free will on another. Love cannot be rushed or forced, and nor can it have burdens placed on its back such as having someone else decide for you. Get to know someone gradually first before jumping into marriage or a committed relationship with someone you don't know.

There are those rare cases where someone has deliberately raced out and nabbed the person they want to marry and it's worked out, but generally you cannot push or force someone to be with you. It will only be met with resistance and disenchantment. During the rare times this has worked is because both people were physically attracted to one another, but a connection based on lust does not always go the distance. A physical attraction is connected to a lust attraction, because you don't know this person well enough to be in love with them. The person's physical exterior beauty and looks blinds one to the truth about them. Having some measure of physical attraction at first is a good start, but being attracted to one's exterior does not guarantee personality chemistry. Eventually the lust filled physical attraction begins to wane if there aren't common interests, communication styles, and similarities between one another. The connections that began as a one-night stand or a physical attraction that have stood the test of time were because both partners had similar interests, values, and communication styles outside of that.

Imagine that ten years can go by and yet no lover has presented themselves to you. If most of your thoughts during those ten years are expecting this lover wondering when they will surface, then this prevents it from happening. It's one of the many laws of the universe in the way that things come about. At the same time, you do not necessarily need to be a passive observer putting in zero effort. If you stumble upon someone on social media, or at the gym, the grocery store, or anywhere and they interest you, then smile and say hello. See where that "hello" can go. Even if it goes nowhere, it at least gets your energy out there in a positive way. This would seem like common sense, but you would be surprised how tongue-tied two people can be when they're both attracted to one another. They feel that it's one sided or part of their imagination. They worry that the other person would never be interested in someone like them. They might feel that the person is out of their league. You don't want to spend the rest of your life wondering if something could've formed with a potential mate if only one or the both of you made a move.

Those who are single and struggling to find love want to know if there is some magic secret to attracting in love. Be a good person and allow that to shine outwardly. Improve yourself on all levels. This means feeling truly whole and loving all that you are. It is accepting all parts of you especially the uncomfortable parts. It is raising your self-esteem into a warrior like confidence that you are content being alone. This is not to be confused with being lonely.

Loneliness and being comfortable alone are two different scenarios. You are in a perfect space of peace. Only when you love yourself in this grand way can you be more than ready for the soul that matches that kind of vibration. Of course, you will have the occasional low periods in life as everyone does. It's human nature to experience ups and downs. You will have those random feelings of low self-esteem or feel tender about the way you look or certain parts of your personality. Optimism attracts in a love partner more than negativity.

Both good and bad people attract in potential love partners everyday. Relationship partners have no prejudice when it comes to the type of person it chooses to get involved with. Good people also get involved with bad people. They might ignore the red flags when seeing this new person through the haze of romance. The reality dawns on them, as they are knee deep in the relationship.

When you meet for the first time, you're secretly looking to see if it's a potential match, marriage partner, date, or even friendship. When there are more meetings or regular conversations with the person after that, then you know that you both like each other enough to get together. You soon start to get a sense over time as to how you want to define the connection. This is whether it's a friendship or if it's a more serious relationship potential, dating, friends, friends with benefits, or the romantic kind of love.

Love is something that takes time to happen and build. If you're immediately in love with someone after you meet them for the first time, then you're not in love, but in lust. There's no way you can love someone you don't know in a deep way. If you've been with them a year and you know their quirks, flaws, challenges, and yet you still love them, then it is real love.

Your Spirit team would never plant your only potential soul mate in one state and then let you lose out on love because you had to move to an entirely different state. There are many potential soul mates, men and women, who could fulfill you spiritually, emotionally, and physically. They are waiting for you in every city, occupation, and social group you might possibly choose to be in at some point in your life.

Forcing love to happen pushes it further away. It brings up fear that it won't happen and frustration that it isn't happening. This energy repels others whether it's a potential partner or someone you're dating. It puts stress and strain on a relationship with its intensity of trying to keep the connection going out of an obsession to hold onto them. The reasons behind this behavioral reaction often have to do with psychological build up from childhood of losing something you wanted whether physically or metaphorically. It can also point to having been denied love growing up, which breeds co-dependence. The other reason is that you've become so excited to have a new love partner that it feels as if you found the one and don't want to lose them. You overcompensate to the point of smothering the other person, or by becoming completely co-dependent that it begins to suffocate them. The other partner ends up retaliating angrily, pulling away, or ending the connection altogether. This could be applied to someone who isn't normally co-dependent by nature. A great deal of independent detached professionals announced that the times they have rare co-dependent feelings rise are only while in a love relationship.

When you develop strong feelings for someone

you've recently met, then this is a combination of lusting after them or falling in love with the idea of them, but it will not necessarily equate to long-term love. True love is developed over time for someone. The more you bond with them and appreciate all aspects of them, then the more love can develop. Take the time and get to know someone before jumping into something serious.

You're on a hamster wheel when you continue to repeat the same patterns that lead nowhere. You continue to attract in the same types of mates, or you have no forgiveness in your heart with a past flame. The mate that is the keeper and the one you'll end up with for good is often the one that's different than what you're used to. That is if you can break the karmic cycle of attracting in the same types of mates that add toxicity to your vicinity. Forgive yourself and any past lovers that have caused you ill will. Otherwise these obstructions can prevent a new connection from entering the picture and blossoming out of the dating stages. You cannot force someone to change and suddenly want you, since you cannot force anyone to do what they don't want to do. Never wait around for someone who is unsure about you.

When it comes to matters of love, your guides and angels will put particular soul mate choices in your path intended to connect with you, but then it is up to you and/or this other person to notice it and act on it. They work with the other person's guides to guide that person toward you, while your own guides are guiding you towards them. That's quite a bit of guiding going on behind the scenes in hopes that both parties notice. They'll get you in the room alone together to face each other, but then it's up to the both of you to do the rest of the work. If neither of you do, then it's back to the drawing board for both sets of guides to continuously work to orchestrate the meeting again and again in hopes that action will be taken. This can only go on for so long before the moment passes, and neither is able to keep the orchestration from happening. At that point a lost opportunity has passed for both parties.

Some guides and angels might agree to show up at a certain juncture of someone's life, such as when major life changes are taking place. They leave once it's calmed down and heavenly help is no longer needed for that circumstance. A spirit guide may be sent to you to assist in preparing you for a particular love relationship partner, or to help you find a specific job where you will learn valuable lessons and skills at in order to utilize later in your personal and/or professional life. Once you and this love partner have connected or you obtained the job you desired, then that particular guide will leave.

Some people have made poor choices out of being deeply in love with someone. Heaven applauds love feelings for another person, but they know one of the side effects of intense obsessive love could fog up your psychic vision and divine connection. This can contribute to you making choices you might not have ordinarily done if those rose-colored glasses weren't tightly on.

Some people have been in a love situation where

they were in love with someone who wasn't as in love with them back. This continues until they find out they were being taken advantage of by that partner. They look back and start to recall the many red flags and Divine signs offered to them about this new prospect. Those signs had been in front of them all along, but because they were in the deep blinding haze of being in this kind of love attraction they failed to notice it or brushed it off. When you're that in love with someone you let them get away with murder, until they react cruelly to you in a way that snaps you back to reality. You realize you knew all along they were wrong for you, but you had been deceived by the dark ego.

CHAPTER NINE

Love and Relationships

When two people merge into the right healthy committed loving union, both of the lights in their souls expand and their vibrations rise. There is no limit to what you are able to accomplish individually while in that soul connection. Love is the main reason all are here. People gravitate towards this concept because deep down most everyone longs to have that kind of a connection if they don't already have it. Most everyone has made that one bond with somebody that pulls you out of yourself completely. Some have that one great love that is never experienced again, while others move through life and never connect with another human soul in an intensely deep way. This is about reciprocated relationships and not unrequited ones.

Unrequited connections are where you have a crush or romantic interest in someone who does not share the same feelings and attraction for you. It can be someone you are in a relationship with who either was never fully into you and settled, or their feelings shifted over the course of the relationship where they no longer have romantic feelings for you. Love relationships experience peaks and valleys, so there will be moments when you both feel as if you're stuck in a rut. This is why relationships take work and effort to continue to keep it interesting, passionate, and thriving.

A requited deep soul connection is where you understand one another more than any other experience you've had with anybody else. It is the kind of union that you never forget, and nor does it ever go away no matter how much you attempt to disregard it. This is the kind of rare soul connection that leaves you haunted by it decades later long after it ends. Your mind always drifts back to that profound tie you had with them. It is one that is never repeated with anyone else. The relationship might not have lasted due to various factors, but often times it's something trivial where one or the both of you allowed your ego to rule your life. When you use little ego, then circumstances function with minimal issues and relationships end up lasting.

The ego is selfish and makes decisions based on self-centeredness that can result in crumbling a union. There is a great deal of self-centeredness in the world today, which is why many struggle to keep relationships going. Before the technological age people were staying married or together their entire lives. Today they're out the door at the slightest sign of it becoming dull or antagonistic. No one usually leaves their long-term job that abruptly, but they have no problem walking away from deeper soul connections.

Selfishness is one of the top causes of relationship sabotage. Selfishness comes from the dark part of your ego. There are varying shades of the ego that range from the light to the dark. The light side of your ego believes in yourself, loving all that you are and having confidence. Relationships require selflessness, which is a quality lacking in today's modern-day world in general, let alone in a love relationship. The ego wants what it desires, even if it triggers damage to a deep soul connection. Soul connections are no accident, but are predestined and determined to make contact with one another this lifetime. A soul mate is a soul connection that pushes your buttons and helps you positively change and grow. Soul mate soul connections assist in one's personal and spiritual growth.

It takes me a long time to come around, but all of my romantic connections have always been forceful and intensely close. This is what happens when you merge in with a love addict. I use the term love addict loosely and in an exaggerated way to imply that I love being in love and being in positive love relationships. The true meaning of the love addict is someone who is in love with the intoxicating high of the initial getting to know someone part, but then once it grows familiar they discard them and move onto the next victim. I've never done that, but rather have grown stronger and more connected with the one I'm with.

The reason it has taken me time in the past to come around is because I've never jumped into a relationship with anyone on a whim. I've taken my love relationships seriously including the coming together part. I need to be sure about them before I commit, because when I do it's for life. However, in the past, I had found those that rushed the commitment were just as rushed to end it. They did this with all those they were with; therefore, do not take love relationships seriously. It is impossible to be with me and not believe it's going to be deep or intense, because it will be. It's just the way it is. The love continues to grow more concentrated as time goes by. If a connection moves into superficiality or distrust, then it will break apart. Have zero tolerance for superficiality in love. Have the mantra of putting in all or nothing. This means you put in 110% into whatever you choose to commit to or don't bother. Don't waste energy on something that you only have half an interest in because it will show.

I can psychically see what is going on underneath and what is unsaid with someone. This has its positives and negatives. The positives are that it tells me what the other person needs. The negatives are when you see something that can make you question who you're with. One of the worst places to be is in a loveless relationship. This squeezes out all traces of oxygen and ultimately brings about suffocation. It is one of the worst love crimes you can commit next to cheating and abuse of any kind.

Those in healthy long-term love relationships report to being happier, calmer, more motivated, and less stressed in their life in general than those who are single. Note the word, "healthy", because being in a drama ridden love relationship, or unrequited one-sided love connection, is just as bad on your health than being addicted to a toxic substance. You might as well be single and develop a healthy social life instead.

Long term love relationships between two people facing in the same direction that have each other's backs tend to be less depressed, have less anxiety, and lowered blood pressure than those struggling alone with no social support system or a love partner for life. The loving soul connection motivates both parties to accomplish more in their life. They tend to live longer happier lives, rather than short miserable ones. The immense benefits in a healthy long-term love relationship are endless. There is no telling what both partners can accomplish while in a loving partnership.

This is not intended to imply that in order to be happy that everyone should jump into a long-term love relationship. There are some people who are not cut out for it, are not ready for it, or they genuinely prefer to be alone and single by choice. They are perfectly happy being single.

It is unwise to jump into a love relationship when you're not in the right space to be in one. It is also not fair to the person you're pushing to get involved with when you're not ready. If they're pushing you and you're not ready, then it is reckless to go along with it knowing that they want what you do not want.

To an extent, realizing your dreams first before getting into a love relationship is ideal, but if you wait for that to happen, then you might be waiting forever. The right partnership gives you that push to conquer your goals by giving you the space and freedom to explore your dreams. Without love within or without, then one's talents and accomplishments mean nothing. Love is the reason all are here bridging souls in one long thread of interconnectedness.

When an entertainer receives an award, nine times out of ten they mostly include their love mate in the speech. Some even go as far as to say how much their mates love is instrumental. Their lover's immense loyalty and support means the world to them. This is because they are aware of how the person closest to them has been their biggest support system and fan than any other. It's a stronger love than any fan because it's personal. This love partner knows who they truly are behind closed doors rather than the persona that the public thinks of them to be like.

How will you know if your relationship has served its purpose or if it is at the end of its tenure? If you have to ask, then it's over. Preoccupying oneself over whether or not a relationship has run its course indicates that you've already got one foot out the door. When doubt exists in your mind, then this is what shall come to you. Letting go of anyone or anything means you first let go of it in your heart. Once that happens, then the energy is activated and heads in that direction without you realizing it. This same process is applied to attracting in a love partner. You feel it in your heart that the love partner is already here. Use your imagination and visualize that it is in motion by believing with cheerful might that it is here now.

No matter how many love experiences gone bad it is worth the risk to open up one's heart to allow love in again, otherwise a missed opportunity can take place. When your heart has been bruised and battered, you subconsciously put up a wall that makes you inaccessible to anyone, even the right one. The warmth is what the right one will be drawn into and not the hostility. It can take a long time after one heart breaking connection has ended before you safely drop that wall of horror to allow someone new in.

When it comes to a love partner, one assumes this person has their back. They are merging spiritually, mentally, emotionally, and physically with this person on all levels. It is considered a big deal to give all of oneself in that way. When your life mate cheated on you, or was physically or verbally abusive, then it can be difficult to reach a place of forgiveness, although it is necessary for you to heal and truly move on.

The world is suffering where love relationships are concerned. This is an ego-based planet that includes ego-based pursuits, which have taken precedence over merging a duo in a beautiful long-term supporting love relationship. The ego contributed to the downfall of relationships. It's the ego that will jump into a relationship quickly and end it recklessly, or the ego will avoid a connection altogether as it dislikes feeling tied down.

When you fall in love, this releases the hormones dopamine and oxytocin. These are feelings that create an overall sense of positive well-being. You're basically high on life! You're suddenly focused and energetic able to accomplish things that you had previously put aside before you fell in love. This is also why being in love and having a love partner is beneficial to your heart, health, and overall well-being. It's also why those who are in love with you can stop at nothing to get you or be with you. This is because in essence love is like a drug. It gives them that natural high where they'll stop at nothing to obtain. The danger of this is that you may be in love with someone who doesn't share those feelings. There is nothing worse than being in love with someone and they're denying it because they're not interested. You'll notice that it doesn't necessarily detour someone from giving up. They will grow miserable or depressed not being able to be with you. Someone might start lashing out or resort to stalking behavior to get as close to you as possible.

There is no fixed formula for making a true unconditional relationship work since it's a mutually agreed upon and understood formula made by both parties. Unconditional relationships are also not 100% accurate, because unconditional means without condition, and you have conditions when in a relationship. You have conditions that your partner doesn't cheat on you. Right there you now love with conditions. But you can get as close as possible to unconditional love while easing up on issues. Unconditional love is a difficult trait to reach. Everyone places conditions on love to one extent or another. You want someone who is loyal, in it for the long haul and sticks around. As soon as you have the lists, then you love with conditions. If you can get pretty close to unconditional, then that is miraculous.

Love can come close to perfection when all of its imperfections are loved and accepted. Be honest with yourself and with others surrounding your intentions. Follow the wisdom of being authentic and real.

Deep down at the soul's core, the soul desires love, companionship, and commitment. The poor influences over the course of one's life confuse that craving with wanting more selfish self-gratifying longings. It has been taught that there is always an easy way out.

When two people merge into a healthy committed loving relationship, both of the lights in their souls expand and their vibrations rise. You know the meaning of the word God while in a healthy committed love relationship. Love and joy are what lifts you into that space. There is no limit to what both people are able to accomplish individually while in that match.

Being in love is a thrilling, joyful, and exciting feeling that only those who have experienced understand the depths it can reach. This is why so many people long to be in a love relationship or have a lover, because they crave that consistent feeling of happiness that the experience brings. In essence, when you are in love with someone, it is the same feeling as having a crush. Crushes never seem to be as intense and profound as they are when you're a teenager.

You've likely felt those strong intense crushing feelings over someone who has no idea you feel that way. You wonder if you have a shot at obtaining them or if they even feel the same way. The idea of having a crush sounds exotic initially, but they're called crushes because they can crush and hurt you emotionally. This is especially the case if the person you have a crush on doesn't return those feelings.

It may be a loveless world, but there are still a great many souls coming together in relationships everyday within the confinement of it. You cannot ditch love entirely, because love is present beneath the layers of all souls regardless if they choose to find ways to access it or not. Love never dies in this sense. You can say you want to focus on work or on yourself, but the bottom line is when a relationship is intended to happen, it will come about unexpectedly regardless if it messes up with your goals to achieve. You can still succeed while in a relationship. Being in the right connection motivates you to accomplish more and reach higher heights, so it's a win-win.

Cuddling, hugging, and touching have immense therapeutic properties. These acts assist to bring down your cortisol levels more rapidly than anything else. When you engage in these activities with someone, or your romantic partner, it assists in lightening the load or dissolving traces of unhappiness, stress, or upset. It raises your vibration and boosts oxytocin levels, which is the love drug hormone that calms your entire body and expands the soul's light. Even if you don't have a love partner, then hugging a friend or a pet can offer the same benefits.

Being physically touched and kissed repeatedly is like oxygen to me. It has the same endorphin release one gets through exercise. I am a walking love bug Casanova after all, which in the past has been a handful or detrimental when I placed it in the hands of the passion-less, the unromantic, or the non-committal.

Partaking in love activities such as regular touch can open up your clair channels to receive clearer guidance and messages from above in this state. Being in love releases the dopamine and oxytocin hormones. What have erupted are upbeat feelings that create an overall sense of positive well-being. You're basically high on life! You're more focused and energetic able to accomplish things that you had previously put aside before you experienced Earth's saving miracle called love. Love is like a drug, but a healthy one that gives you a natural high that no vice, cigarette, drink, drug, or bad food can offer or reach.

Like the song, remember to let your love flow like a mountain stream…

CHAPTER TEN

Love is a Battlefield

The relationships you have with others make up a big part of your life. These relationships can positively or negatively affect who you are and the overall state of your well-being. This is why you will want to ensure that you work on raising your vibration in order to invite in higher vibration souls into your vicinity. Avoid or distance yourself from those who are harmful and toxic to you. It can be challenging for someone with a low vibration to connect with a high vibration person, because the high vibration person can sense someone who is not of integrity or who has a low vibration. They will steer clear of someone with a low vibration. High vibration souls are extra sensitive and avoid participating in situations that will wreak havoc on their system. This includes being around toxic people.

When you get close to a high vibration person, you will discover they tend to mostly be friendly, compassionate, loving, and supportive people. The reason we say mostly is because they are ultra-sensitive. If someone crosses them or they sense harsh tampering energy on their soul's system, then they may grow frustrated and lash out, or they take off staying far away from the low vibration soul. This is the fight or flight response that those with higher psychic sensitivities have. The way that spirit beings are attracted to the light around any soul, the high vibration human soul is attracted to those with a large light as well.

To those that know a high vibration soul personally, they will say they're good people and not gossips or prone to following the crowd to fit in. They are into improving or taking care of themselves on some level. They are confident and comfortable with being alone and rarely fall into bouts of loneliness. If they ever do, then it comes and goes quickly. It is not part of their basic human nature. When the soul is operating from its higher self, then loneliness doesn't exist in the equation. Loneliness is a trait that comes out of the human condition.

This isn't to say that high vibration people do not drop their vibration or feel lonely from time to time. On average their vibration is dropping and rising all throughout the day. They are aware when it drops, and they begin the immediate work to raise it again naturally. They know what to avoid and what will negatively affect them in order to do this. Whereas someone that functions primarily with a low vibration tends to stay on that level until they have that awakening moment where they realize they need to make healthy life changes.

The human soul that has repetitive negative critical statements to say about someone is operating from a low vibration. A high vibration soul is not the one who congregates around the water cooler to gossip and spew negative words. They're the ones that distance themselves from that. This isn't out of shyness, but because they're not attracted to energy drainers. They don't need it or crave it on any level.

Feelings of loneliness will make you feel empty and miserable while lowering your vibration in the process. It can come upon someone who is bored, feels a low sense of self-worth, or craves a higher amount of social stimulation from others. Another person cannot fill these feelings up since this is something that needs to be developed from within you. A high vibration person operates from a higher space and usually does not desire curing someone of their boredom or boosting up someone's self-esteem. This doesn't mean the high vibration person does not desire a love relationship. They crave someone who is on their wavelength and of a like mind. They may complain that the suitors they connect with tend to be of a lower vibration. Low vibration suitors might cheat, are non-committal, or emotionally unavailable. They might be someone heavily addicted to a harsh toxin such as drugs or alcohol, and are uninterested in reducing or eliminating it.

High vibration people are catches for someone who wants to go the distance in a love relationship. They attract in others of varying vibration levels including those on a lower vibration. Getting involved with someone with a permanent low vibration is not suitable, as it can affect you and drop your own vibration in the process. It's like a fitness guru who is into nutrition and health, and yet they fall for and get involved romantically with someone who drinks alcohol in large quantities daily. It can be someone interested in going to museums and art galleries, and yet they get involved with someone who loves hitting the clubs or bars on a weekly basis. Once they are both deep into the connection, they secretly wonder how they ever got to together to begin with since their life choices are completely different from one another. They might have been compatible from an astrological, soul mate, personality standpoint, yet they partake in opposing activities. This can become frustrating from both sides if neither can accept their differences. It is something that should have been addressed in the early dating stages. Human beings are trained to put on their best face forward when meeting someone. This is a sense of deception, because you can only keep your best face going for so long before your true colors reveal itself to one another.

There would be a running joke in the past with whoever I was dating that I was revealing all the worst aspects of me immediately. This natural method of mine made those potential suitors even more attracted to me. I wasn't hiding anything and allowed it to all hang out on the surface. I joked, "If you can survive this, then we'll get along really well."

This kind of openness rarely pushed them away or turned them off, but instead ended up having the opposite effect. Each of the potential suitors would later say, "You started out by showing me your worst traits, but as I got to know you I realized how amazingly compassionate and loving you are. You mask it with all this other stuff."

I explained I wasn't masking anything, but being my true self by revealing all facets of me up front. This method is the reverse from the norm where you're trained to put on the deceptive face to lure someone into your vicinity. Six months pass and the other person feels deceived as they learn things about you they're not comfortable with. Those who put on a deceptive face up front eventually discover that they have been found out.

I've heard others say that you treat a romantic date as if it is a job interview. This means you show the best parts of you up front. While this is true for a job interview it's not true for a romantic date. This isn't to say that you behave like a pig as you're getting to know this date, unless being a pig is your natural self. You put on your best face for a job interview, because when you are working at a job you're wearing a different professional hat that you maintain while at that job. It's a hat that does not include your personal life or who you truly are. A potential romantic partner needs to see and know the real you. The real soul mate that is intended for you will love all parts of you, as you will equally with them.

You check certain aspect traits of yourself at the door when you walk into work to focus only the job you've been hired to do. If this interferes with certain belief systems, then it's time to find a job that jives with your morals. You keep your professional and personal life separate at work. You date someone because you're looking to discover if you and the date will be a match for a potential long-term love relationship. If you're hiding important aspects of yourself with this date and you grow closer and deeper with them, soon enough these hidden aspects will come out. When it comes out, your mate will see it as dishonest. For those who have experienced this, they understand that it's a total blow to not have known the person they were seeing was a certain way until far in with them.

Joining into the most perfect romantic duo you will find that issues arise both big and small. What ensures a successful partnership is that both people love and respect each other enough to compromise. The ego does not like cooperation. It only wants what it wants and does not care what you desire. Relationships can go the distance when both people temper their ego and work together as a team communicating effectively. Modern day love relationships are happening during a time of narcissism running high. This has caused love relationships to be massively short lived or to not come about at all.

Everyone and everything are made up of energy.

This dictates the kinds of people you will attract into your area depending on the energy you give off. If you're someone who is always negative, then you will bring in those who are the same. The ones that find they're stuck with a negative person will find a way to break away from the connection when they develop the nerve.

Love and relationships are obsolete to the ego. The ego wants control, and this is witnessed with the current state of love relationships. By the time the Internet and social media became prominent, it was discovered that there are more single people than those in serious love relationships for the first time in Earth's history at that point. Many prefer hooking up with someone rather than developing a meaningful connection with them.

Technology has killed the long-term love relationship. Before the Internet, social media, and dating phone apps existed, human souls took their connections seriously. They never took them for granted the way many do now. When they would meet someone pre-technology days, they took that person seriously because there was no Internet or phone app to quickly log on and try and meet a replacement. They were grateful for the rare connections they formed. They cared about them and were interested in making it strong and long lasting.

Social media, dating sites, and phone apps are a candy store to the ego. The ego knows that if there is one tiny flaw in someone else that it doesn't like, then it would just log right back onto the app and chat away with more strangers in hopes of finding a replacement or at least a one-night stand. Before the rise in technology, people did not have that luxury. They took those they met seriously and developed long term love relationships and friendships for life. Their egos didn't have it that easy to leave everyone on a whim and start chatting around again online or on a phone app. The ego is unable to connect with one person throughout the duration of its Earthly life. It will find excuses to sabotage connections with others, give you reasons to cheat, or prompt you to govern your life from a place of selfishness. On the flipside, someone ruled by their ego full time is not someone ready to be seriously dating or getting involved with another person on a considerable level anyway.

There is nothing wrong with not desiring a love relationship. Some may not want one for good reason. Perhaps they're in no position to be in a love relationship. They might not be able to remain faithful to one person or they are battling addictions. They're uncomfortable with love, emotionally unavailable, or they're not where they want to be in life. You can still find meaningful relationships with others outside of monogamous love connections such as friendships, colleagues, acquaintances, and family members.

When you join another soul in this life, you are forming a partnership and a team. Teamwork involves working together efficiently as if it is a growing and prosperous business. Each soul brings something to the table that the other soul might lack. You and this partner are both Teacher and Student where you switch and reverse the roles.

When two people have gone into business together and face issues with their company, they don't immediately walk away from it. They sit down together to brainstorm ways of building it and making it stronger. It is interesting that others do this with work, but that it's not considered to do with their relationships.

In the end, the soul longs for companionship or a love relationship on some level. It wants to grow older with someone they feel a strong attraction for. It is the ego that does not desire this. The ego prefers freedom to hook up with random people or not fully commit to anyone at all. Technology and the media have both destroyed the possibility of deep long-lasting love relationships. It's not the technological gadget and the media that did that, but it is the individual ego working in the media, or who has access to technology that did. You give an ego power such as a fun and curious toy to play with and they will break it sooner or later.

I've received cases from those who hook up regularly. After talking with me about it, they admit to doing it for attention and love. In these cases, they expressed that they've been perpetually single and desire companionship, but that it has not surfaced. In the interim, they seek it out through meaningless hook ups. There is no judgment if this is what someone chooses to do, so don't misunderstand if you enjoy hooking up with others. What this is about is the common complaint expressed from someone who hook-ups regularly that they tend to feel even lonelier not long afterwards. Like any addiction or drug, they log back onto the phone app or website to find another hook up to temporarily satisfy their need for love. The suitors they connect with for a hook up mean nothing to them. It's a cycle they struggle with breaking. The others who hook up do so because they want to. They do not want to feel tied down to one person and crave variety. The others who do it are driven by a strong carnal sexual nature to begin with.

Technology is cold, aloof, and distant. This is how others are in the dating sphere. There is a detachment in texting and chatting that translates to how relationships function today. Technology has trained the ego to not develop emotional intelligence nor to dive beneath the surface.

Long-term monogamous love relationships are possible to have despite how it might seem. There are many happy couples that have gone the distance and last until the end. They are loving and compassionate with one another. They communicate regularly and support each other on all levels. Others around see them as a power couple, a success story, and one to dream and thrive for. In a successful love relationship, it is you and this other person against the world. You understand one another's strengths and weaknesses. You fill in the gaps that help one another grow and prosper. You take care of each other until the end of your days in this lifetime.

Everyone is in survival mode and it can feel unusual to the soul to have to endure difficult times alone without any support. This is where you ask God and your Spirit team for intervention during those times of struggle. Your team is loyal to you and present for you beyond measure.

Avoiding relationships does not help your soul grow. Necessary tools are gained when you join in any kind of connection with someone else, regardless if it's love, friendships, colleagues, or even acquaintances. After the rise in technology, it became incredibly difficult for human beings to connect with one another in relationships.

You desire a love companionship, but have found it impossible to obtain leaving you frustrated and dejected. To an extent there is a certain measure of pickiness. Technology made everyone a star, which expanded the human ego. They have the long lists of what they won't accept in someone else without any room for compromise or movement. If one is that strict over every little thing, then they'll be looking at a life of single-dom.

Others refuse to date a quality person who might either be too young, too old, too short, or too tall and so on. While some are looking for some perfect Adonis or Barbie looking person that appears as if they jumped out of a model magazine. These are all ridiculous qualities to have on one's list of what they're looking for. You rule out quality soul mates due to trivial fetish traits and therefore end up single indefinitely. Most of the time people end up with those they would not have necessarily been attracted to. There are cases where someone has a strong attraction for tall brunettes, but in the end they find that the person they ultimately fall deeply in love with for life is a short blonde.

There are common sense qualities that most do not want in a potential long-term love relationship. These are traits such as you don't want to be involved with someone who has a drinking problem, does drugs, is emotionally unavailable, is violent, or has a tendency to cheat and stray. At the same time for some people, when you're in a healthy long-term relationship, then that reduces or zaps away the desire to consume negative toxins and addictions in high quantities. The reason is real authentic love between two people raises both of your vibrations. When your vibration is high, then you don't crave or desire toxins. You are also less addicted to those substances. I've also personally found this to be the case ending up with those that battled those kinds of addictions, but they were reduced and diminished initially during our honeymoon phase. Part of this is that love raises the Dopamine chemical in your brain that makes you feel good. When you feel good naturally such as in a love high, then you're not craving toxins to get that artificially. You don't need it anymore, because you're already getting the chemical high through love.

An addicted person may grow bored or start to feel inadequate while in the love connection. They soon reach for the addiction in hopes it will remove those negative feelings. For some, they may fall into that addictive behavior, but they're absolved in it far less than when they're single and unhappy. If you're someone battling addictions to something, then it is often likely you'll fall back into that toxic path while in this healthy loving long-term relationship. This is because the love relationship can only sustain that for so long before it is no longer in the newness category. The honeymoon love high will eventually wear off for that individual, then the hard work comes in. Many leave the relationship when it gets to that point, because they want to continue feeling good and will seek out another new person to get it from.

Quality suitors want someone who is decent, cool, and a loving, supportive partner like friend. They desire someone who is in the connection with them and has the intention of going at it together for life. This is someone you can freely talk to and open up with about anything. It is someone that loves you and who you love right back without hesitation. It is not one person always being the listening ear, but it is a give and take. Even when you do not feel like it, you drop everything to listen to your partner. This is why love relationships are work. You have to put in the work as if it is your job, except you love this job because you love this person.

Some of the highest vibration qualities that exist are activities such as mutual hugging, cuddling, loving, and touching. The soul longs for air to breathe and these actions awaken your soul. Perhaps you had a lover who reached over to hold your hand and you know how amazing your soul felt to be that close to them. It feels as if you're soaring above the clouds and all you feel and know are love. You discover what matters while here and that is love. Love yourself first and you will be closer to inviting in someone who is the same.

CHAPTER ELEVEN

Seeking Love Through External Validation

It can be challenging to find any love essence on a planet that is primarily ego driven. Reading stories laden in protesting gossip has no love within it. Focus on the positives of a situation, rather than dwelling on matters that are desperately out of your hands. Take the stance of an egoless angel who sees the love and positives of a circumstance. They understand that the way things are laid out is designed and soul contracted for a reason, even if the dark part of your ego has a tough time coming to grips with that reality. When you detach from the noise and drama of the bitterness in the hearts of those on the planet, then your consciousness is raised enough that it allows God's love filled light to come rushing in. This is followed by the higher Universal truth coming into view.

Resistance does nothing to move humanity forward. Having understanding, tolerance, compromise and meeting in the middle is what bridges the wide gap. This is the space where Universal love resides. Resistance is having a tantrum that creates a block stemming from the darkness of ego. It's stubborn and unwilling to compromise, which keeps others separated and divided. Resistance is not interested in working with others. It's defiant, it's rigid, it struggles, it impedes. Positive energy doesn't flow through having resistance. Resistance is restricting, which blocks Divine love communication from sifting into one's consciousness. There is no love or God existing in resistance. This doesn't mean you're siding or condoning what you believe to be bad behavior in someone else. It does mean you are taking the angelic perspective into peering into the complicated composites of the person you disagree with through love and not anger. This can also be applied to interpersonal connections.

The opposite of resistance is peace, cooperation, compromise, and meeting in the middle. One is more likely to listen to and warm up to someone that negotiates peacefully to find common ground over being aggressively stubborn and resistant. The answers can be found in that centered space where peace, joy, and love reside. When has war, fighting, anger, and resistance won the collective over? It's created more friction, more war, more anger, and more fighting. The ones falling into that venue are the ones protesting that it's getting worse and it's everyone else, but they're not taking the higher view to see how they've contributed negatively to that energy.

Absorbing yourself in negativity doesn't help anyone. It's understandable to be concerned about issues you were brought here to improve, but to dwell on negativity is called drama. No one likes it except those that stir it up. Residing in drama is the opposite of love. Focus on action that will improve a concern while debunking those that stir up spectacle and negativity. Regularly ranting on social media at others is not action, but toxic drama and gossip. If you preach about love or the light all over your social media, then walk the talk in all areas of your life.

For centuries, the Internet, technology, and social media never existed. People lived fulfilling deep and profound lives in person with others without any issues.

If all you care about is being loved by others in-person or online, then you risk getting carried down in that tide of caring about what someone else thinks. You can always count on Heaven to love you. When you are in the mode of appreciation and reciprocating that love, then you are in harmony with the Divine. When you lose yourself to what it means to truly love, and you despise those that have disagreeing opinions from you, then you disconnect further away from the source that the Light resides in.

Having true compassion and tolerance is by embracing and including those who are in opposition. It's the way to begin the process of bridging the gap of divisiveness laid out by the individual ego. This is a trait that the planet desperately needs to learn. They've always been divisive, but now it's at an alarming rate due to the way word travels through the Internet waves.

In order to walk the talk and walk in someone else's shoes, you have to be able to metaphorically walk in someone else's shoes. You have to know what it's like to be inside their consciousness. Otherwise, you'll never understand or have empathy to what they are experiencing. A great actor can do this able to play a vile monster of a character while not losing sight of their humanity. Many actors have acknowledged that yes the character is evil in the moviegoer's eyes, but they cannot personally look at the character as being evil while playing it. They have to understand the character's viewpoint and find the humanity no matter how monstrous that person is to others.

Social media is a playground for the ego. There are different measures of how the darkness of ego comes out in social media. Some of it is worse than others. You know what is along the lines of what is and what isn't. Unless social media is being used positively to bring light to important issues, then it tends to be used for some form of attention. It depends on how extreme or severe the need for attention is that it can be corrupting, which ultimately delays and holds that soul back from true accomplishment.

Human souls crave love, appreciation, and acknowledgement. The soul wants to be loved because it knows it flourishes when being radiated with love. It cannot breathe without love, so it will do whatever it takes to obtain that love in anyway it can. It craves God's all-encompassing love, which is lost in the dark banal physical existence. To put that kind of demanding expectation on other people to fulfill is putting too much burden on others who cannot satisfy that unnerving requirement.

The way to accelerate life on Earth towards Utopia is if every person on the planet resided in their soul's true nature, which is in a state of all love, joy, and peace. It's virtually impossible for millions of souls to exude that state around the clock in today's ego driven physical designed modern world governed by the darkness of ego. It is counterproductive to their true nature, so people live under constant stress as a result.

Choose to rise above negativity by showing some beautiful poised class. Stay centered in grace and love despite any whirlwind of darkness surrounding you. Nothing is truly as bad as it seems. When a line is crossed, then you graciously intercept it by focusing on solutions rather than creating unnecessary issues. What you focus on will multiply, so you want to make sure it's positive. If you find you fall into the epicenter of negativity, then work on moving past that and in bridging the gap between all souls, including the ones that hold a differing perspective than you.

Look at the positive aspects of a situation or

walk away from it. Divert your attention to the blessings in your life, and steer clear of the intoxicating drama and gossip that attempts to lure you into its sticky trap. It does nothing to help anyone and improves nothing, but contributes more hopelessness to the nonsense.

Warrior of Lights and spiritual helpers contribute their part to spread love around the world in hopes it will raise the Universal consciousness, but it will not be an overnight effort. It will still be centuries of slow-moving progress in baby forward steps to Universal love.

The Divine loves all souls equally and no one is ever ignored even when it feels that way. To Heaven, Earthly life is a blip on the radar and a millisecond compared to eternity. The perspective Spirit has is greater than imagined by the human mind. Experiencing that great love feeling from the Divine begins by increasing your faith and having regular daily prayer or conversations with God. Even if it feels like you're talking to no one, you are heard and responded to at some point. This is where you pick up on the messages and guidance immediately or further down the line. Sometimes you have to endure a rough patch before the light is shown. At the moment when the light appears, you realize why you were kept in a situation longer than you intended to be and then it suddenly all makes sense.

When you're operating in your highest self's state of joy, peace, and love, then that's when you are more able to notice the Divine signs around that you're not alone and that you are loved and looked out for. In the physical world, the ego requires physical concrete material evidence of that love, but the love is felt from within like a great big warm hug. This is part of what having faith entails. The Divine has no judgment and all are loved. There is nothing you can do to rescind that love. Spirit will not suddenly say, "Oh you're hopeless, I'm done with you."

As challenging as it is to believe, even the most heinous human being is loved. It is who the soul is deep inside that is loved. The intention is that the soul learns to reduce, dissolve, and limit operating from the darkness of ego. It is expected to awaken its consciousness to the spiritual reality they are bigger than the limited being they've chosen to confine themselves to. Heaven doesn't say to completely eliminate the darkness of ego, because even the most all loving and compassionate being on the planet will fall into the dark side of the ego on occasion. It's a limited rare occurrence that creeps up infrequently compared to the heinous dark human beings that have chosen to live a life ruled primarily from the darkest depths of their ego.

To sense the encompassing love from the Divine, it is necessary to reduce Earthly distractions in order to raise the voices of Heaven. Participate in a soul detox that includes limiting technological use on certain days, getting out in nature to clear the mind, exercising regularly, reducing toxic foods and drinks, and centering and balancing out your thoughts and feelings.

Don't allow negativity and drama to sway you

from your purpose. You become a way shower and a leader by inspiring and enlightening, as well as remembering to display assertive love and compassion. Don't forget who you are and why you are here. Be a warrior of light who shines so much light and love onto all sides that your body cannot contain it.

A parent disciplines their child out of love in order to differentiate between what they believe to be an acceptable mode of conduct as opposed to a disagreeable one. This isn't to be confused with blatant abuse. There is a difference between discipline and abuse. A good parent faces the student soul in the direction of love at all times.

Don't pay attention to the screaming noise of the ego, but stay centered and balanced in the whirlwind of Heaven's love instead. The truth of your purpose for being lives deep inside you. When you stop to clear away the metaphorical cobwebs and the noise, then focus inward and then above allowing the truth to rise up so you can see it with exceptional Divine clarity.

Being loved feels incredible because it is the one area that all souls desire, even if it seems to manifest itself outwardly in the physical world through disentangled misguided means. You may post one selfie after another on your social media account for external validation that gives you temporary satisfaction. You post another and another constantly seeking out love and affection from anyone willing to give it. The love you receive from that is temporary, so like any drug you experience withdrawals, then wind up using the vice again. You quickly head to your social media account to post away for more adoration in the form of likes, comments, or for anyone interested, even if it's just for yourself.

As with many things in this Earthly life there is a gauge between the healthy and unhealthy. The healthy side is posting selfies to have fun on social media. Done in moderation is a form of self-love, but where it gets into dangerous territory is when it's used all day long every day for external validation from others. This is where you risk bordering on narcissism or the opposite of that which is low self-esteem that manifests into an unstoppable craving of love and admiration from others. God and your Spirit team love you around the clock free of charge. When tuned into the Divine you can access that love knowing that it exists within you.

Narcissism isn't as dangerous as having low self-esteem, but it is toxic in higher amounts. Most everyone can be accused of being narcissist today. If you have a social media account that you post on regularly about what you're up to, then that is a form of narcissism, yet it depends what the content is. Posting stuff about you that can help others will fall into the realms of motivational self-improvement. It's contributing positively towards the betterment of humanity one person at a time. It is encouraging content intended to inspire others or to put a great idea in their mind to act on. Maybe it's to cheer you on to exercise more, or offer awesome healthy related cooking recipes, to delving deeper into higher learning.

Sometimes when you're posting random nothingness one after the other, then you end up spamming people with it. This might be done out of boredom or for driving desire for praise and external validation from others. There is a longing desperation to connect. This is about diving deeper to see if you're falling into perpetual non-productivity to cover up other issues that could be related to loneliness, lack of drive, or any other hidden emotional matter.

Social media helps give the lonely an outlet to connect with the outside world, which to another extent is positive if it gives the soul a healthy boost to engage. If you're a shut in and afraid to leave your house, then social media can help you connect with others from your personal computer or cell phone. In that respect, you are teetering on that fine line of having a healthy outlet to connecting with others to desiring false attention.

The real people that know you in person are the ultimate genuine beings that love you for you, because they are with you no matter what. They know and have seen you in person and they still stick around and remain loyal. There's nothing you could do that could take away that love, which is the closest one can get to unconditional. At the same time, there are people who feel isolated or live that kind of existence and have no authentic in-person relationships. Social media and apps can help give that person access to engage with other people, so long as it doesn't further isolate you from reality or cause depression.

Numerous studies have been conducted over the

years indicating that lower social media usage is good for one's well-being, but higher social media usage has led to a higher rate of anxiety and depression. Those that struggle with social anxiety specifically had a stronger well-being when they engaged positively in social media on a minimal level. However, those that struggle with other anxiety related disorders and/or depression were more likely to overuse social media. Their usage borders on abuse whether it's constantly logging on out of boredom, or the abuse comes out towards others such as in comments, posts, as well as mentally comparing themselves to people. The ones that were comparing themselves tended to post more negative comments. With that said it could be safely understood that all those people that function from the darkness of ego and post negative attacks online are also battling some form of mental health issue. This could easily make sense considering that generally happy people with a stronger well-being state don't usually resort to posting negativity whether in posts, comments or online messages.

This could go even further as you psychoanalyze the human condition. Most human beings desire social interaction including the loneliest shut in of a recluse. If you're shy and find it tough to make genuine in-person friends, then social media can help you come out of your shell a bit. Where this gets into a problem is if your whole life and state of being relies on strangers to prop you up and give you the thumbs up or approval. That puts too much pressure on other people who can't provide that constant validation and love giving to one person indefinitely.

Inevitably you will be let down when you post something one day that doesn't garner that much attention. You wonder if you blew it or went too far or if people had enough of the spamming post. Weeks later you post something else that is #1 with a bullet and you're riding on cloud nine again with all the attention. It makes you feel as if you're a loved celebrity where you are popular for a day. This gives the ego a nice stroking making you feel good…. temporarily. Because if your self-esteem is not in check, it will come crashing down when that validation starts to dissolve all over again. It's a cycle that goes on indefinitely until you wake up and realize how much you've been relying on attention from others on social media to continuously validate you. Some have gone further by wondering whether they want to be on social media anymore, as it's become too much work and a drag to partake in.

You know you've gone too far when you realize you post something nearly every hour of every day and you're not selling a product. This becomes overkill for those that follow you prompting them to like your posts less. What a beautiful awareness level to reach when you can safely say that your desire for praise and attention from strangers on social media no longer matters. This is when you no longer seek love from external sources. You can conjure up that love from within the deepest part of your soul that is aligned with God who is all love.

CHAPTER TWELVE

Divine Soul Love

Connecting with source feels as if you're floating high on life and love. It's like a huge Dopamine rush that happens naturally without having to self-medicate with anything. Imagine being in that state around the clock in Heaven, because that's what it feels like back home. It's just a natural uplifting high.

Humanity is gravely obsessive over their physical appearance because the ego in humankind harshly judges one another by what they look like. The perception of who is considered beautiful or good looking would be vastly different if people saw one another's soul instead of the physical vessel they temporarily inhabit. Relationships would last longer because people would be merging together based on soul attraction rather than physical attraction, even though it's understood that in this world it is physical attraction that helps at first, but that's only the start of coming together. Physical attraction fades no matter how good looking someone is. When you're younger you base the quality of a potential love partner solely on their physical attractiveness to you. As you grow older and more mature, the quality of a potential love partner is based on personality chemistry and the companionship factor. You feel a natural easy soul rapport.

Craving human interaction and social stimulation is something sought out by many, while other people prefer to function alone. When you have a strong connection with God and Spirit, then you never feel lonely. Loneliness is ultimately longing for a connection to fulfill you that can only truly be satisfied by God. To have a mutually reciprocated blissful love union with another person is to know God, because a soul's best qualities are parts of Him.

Since it's sometimes difficult for a human soul to have a connection with God, the ego part of one's self will crave love, attention, and admiration from other people. It's temporarily fulfilling because no one can ever fill that space within you except God. God in this case is not that cliché image of a man with a beard sitting on a chair in the sky. This is the image that non-believers tend to overuse, which has no basis in the reality of the massive energy force that created all that IS.

All souls desire some form of companionship

with at least one person. Some people might disagree, but they do crave some form of a relationship based in love if even through a social circle of friends.

You might be connected to one another through technological devices, but in a distant loveless way. You are not connected to God through those forms. The entire planet is unsettled making it near impossible to sense the Divine energy that way. Your subconscious is aware of it, even if you're not paying attention to it in the present moment. If you're a highly spiritually connected being, then you're versed and readily able to move in and out of the Spirit connection whenever it calls for it.

Looking to the future with optimism you might sometimes find you've been chasing rainbows that evaporate as quickly as the champagne fizzles in your glass. You need not search long and hard for some measure of magic to reveal itself since it's always resided within you. You are loved even when you doubt it, avoid it, shun it and do everything in your power to deny it. When you reach that threshold of completing your Earthly run, the only thing you take with you is love. If you gain anything while here, then remember to love more, give more, and have compassion no matter how unpopular it is. Only then can you truly discover that magic you secretly desire.

More often than not, you agreed to have a physical life for a variety of purposes. Everyone is on the planet with the goal of spreading the three biggest traits aligned with God: Love, joy, and peace. All words affiliated with those three words describe what Heaven is like. You may look around and wonder how humanity grew to be removed from those phenomenal traits, but it is the reason you are here. Life is rough for some and reaching that state of being can be challenging, but it is not impossible.

All souls have access to the deeper parts of their consciousness. When you are born, you are 100% psychic and in tune to all things around you, beyond, and on over to the Other Side. Gradually, your caregivers, peers, and the society you grew up in began to have a larger influence on your human development. They train you on what to like, what not to like, and how to think. The ones who break away from that cycle know they have an important mission or purpose here, even if it's to spread compassion, love, or joy to others in some manner.

When any spirit being in Heaven communicates with you, the tone is direct, full of love, and uplifting, even if they are warning you of danger. They communicate firmly, while your ego communicates with uncertainty, anger, or any other disapproving emotion. Your Spirit team will never advise you to do something that ends up hurting you or someone else. This can be something such as developing a sudden urge to recklessly pack up and move away all of a sudden. It can be leaving a soul mate connection that was intended for you in order to go after someone else. Notice around you whom it might hurt including yourself. Typically, rash decisions tend to come from the ego since the ego is impatient. It believes the grass is always greener elsewhere, but where it currently is.

Every living soul is a descendant of the first man and woman that walked the Earth. No one is separated by color, culture, gender, sexual orientation, or any other factor. The darkness of human ego caused separation from one another. When someone is not evolving, then they view their surroundings and other souls in a limited way. They are uncomfortable with anyone who is different from them being in their vicinity. The ego will grow angry and cause them harm, pain or hatred just because the other person is not an identical clone. The lower evolved self sees this person as threatening, while the higher evolved self views others with understanding, love, acceptance, and compassion.

What others feel God to be is up for individual debate. The higher evolved human souls' sense that in the end that it's all supposed to be about love. The further you stray from love, the more disconnected you are from spirit and God.

Bringing yourself to your natural state is where you see things through the eyes of love. Your higher self requires nothing because everything is as it should be. If a mistake is made, your higher self learns from it with indifferent emotion and moves on. Your higher self efficiently corrects the mistake without drama because it knows that all is well. This is just an Earthly life run and should not have to be so complicated. It becomes complex when you are mired down heavily in physical desires and functions. You have to get a job and go to work to make money to survive. It's understood that this is how physical Earthly life is. You can still go after the physical necessities you require without getting obsessively bogged down in it that it stresses you out or makes you permanently unhappy.

Heaven understands you're going through human experiences they cannot relate to since it is not the world they live in. They reside in a place that is all love, all knowing, uplifting joy, happiness, serenity, and peace. There is no antagonism, bullying, domination, and unkindness where they are.

It doesn't matter what someone believes or does not believe, because God grants all living energy free will choice. The purpose for that is to help your soul learn, grow, and evolve. When you have free will choice, then you are more likely to make mistakes to learn from. You don't learn, grow, and evolve unless you're granted the freedom to choose and experience things for yourself.

Everyone is connected to God because there is no way you cannot be. God has the highest vibration traits possible and imaginable. It is easy to determine who is picking up on the voices of God and who is not. This means when someone exudes high vibration traits such as love, joy, and peace, then they are connected to God in that moment. When you exude traits that are the opposite of that such as hate, pain, negative feelings, and emotions, then you are disconnected from God. What this also means is that someone can be a practicing religious person who goes to Church regularly, or works in a Church, and yet they are unaware they are disconnected from God.

What a spectacular gift it is to have the luxury of

life everlasting. Your life is intended to be about love. Your soul in your body craves this love full time. Say goodbye to the dead part of you, and all that no longer serves your higher good, and welcome in a brand-new Phoenix rising gradually emerging and bursting out at the seams dying to get out and soar into freedom. You are alive, awakened, ignited, and ready for the most incredible ride up ahead. Make everyday count and spread love like you never have before.

No one who has been paying any attention can deny that Earth has been in a permanent state of disarray at the hands of corrupt people. The higher your psychic awareness is, then the more conscious you are of the disintegrating state of the planet. You cannot be in denial of this reality. You can be optimistic that there is serenity up ahead for life on Earth, which is why many sensitive strong loving souls incarnate into an Earthly life. It is in order to help move humanity along towards that goal. The struggle for them is that Earth is not an easy place for them to live on. They are aware of Earth's decay and have great distaste over the toxic behavior of humanity as a whole. When you are conscious of that feeling, then that is a sign that you are called on here to rise up and fight to bring love to Earth. Your goal is to help raise the consciousness of all souls back into its original state of being that is love.

There are no limitations beyond the physical world. The freedom to appear how one chooses back home on the Other Side is limitless. The only thing that doesn't change is the soul's consciousness. The soul's consciousness grows and evolves, but the essence of that soul remains relatively the same, which at its core is all love. If the soul's consciousness hasn't evolved, then it goes through specific training that takes place as a human being having an Earthly life, which is filled with challenges. Earthly life is made up of teachers and students in various levels of spirit evolvement.

The brighter the light is around you, then the easier it is to communicate with those on the Other Side. This light acts as a portal to connect with your Spirit team. They are with you from your Earthly birth until your Earthly death. Upon your human death is when you pass on through the tunnel doorway back home to stand face to face with your Spirit team. Those who work with angels, guides, or any being in Heaven on a grander level tend to have more spirit beings around working with them. Those who have larger purposes to help move humanity forward towards the ultimate goal that is love will also have more guides around helping them with this purpose.

I've forever heard the voices of Spirit since I was a kid. It was never unusual and has perpetually been a part of my everyday life for as long as I can remember. I was having conversations with those I could not see. Sometimes members of my Spirit team speak individually and other times it's in unison or harmony. The voices are slightly different from my own voice, although occasionally it might even sound like my own voice coming in from an alternate Universe. Growing up, I also did not know there was a name for it. It's not like this is studied in schools growing up, although spiritual studies should be a big part of the education system. It is non-denominational and helps in empowering and inspiring every individual to Universal love. It would definitely assist in altering the world for the better by teaching others class etiquette. There would be less negativity and hostile ego bullying, with more love and joy on Earth being exuded.

Spirit beings in Heaven see the light of love within you and ignore the range of wasted emotions, because to them everything will always end up being alright as it should be.

When circumstances grow extra intense around you, then issues or concerns that were doormat rise up to the surface in a big bad way. Use those moments to release anything that doesn't benefit your higher self. Find a spot in quiet nature to detangle and detach from the negative energies you've absorbed. Breathe in the love deeply and exhale out any stresses and concerns giving it to God and your Guide and Angel for positive transmutation.

All souls should utilize shielding methods to keep toxic energies at bay. This can be by saying something like this at least once a day:

"Archangel Michael, thank you for surrounding with me white light. Allowing only the love to penetrate."

Your gut feelings and hunches are connected to having clairsentience. It can sometimes be tricky deciphering what is real and what is imagined. Imagined or fear-based energies are conjured up by the ego and lower self, while Divine communication is uplifting and full of love.

When it's your Guide or Angel, then you will hear the word, "You". It will be direct and immersed in love and optimism. This voice will say something like, "You will obtain that job as you are more qualified than you realize."

The guidance, information, and messages from spirit have high vibration energy to it. It is also filled with uplifting love that assists you or someone else in a positive way. If you are riled up in anger, then that is your ego, since heavenly communication is bathed in calm love even if it's a warning. The chatter in your mind causes confusion and chaos pushing you to act on the voice of ego. If you feel you're receiving messages urging you to create negative disruption in your life, or to hurt yourself, or harm someone else in any fashion, then that is the chatter in your mind and not God. Voices from spirit are direct, optimistic, and filled with compassion and love, even if it's sending you a warning.

Many are usually surprised over the humor that pops in and out at times while talking to Heaven. That's because Heaven is not some stern, harsh, cold place. It's filled with uplifting love, peace, and joy. Those are qualities that all beings in Heaven exude. They are bathed in those energies, which equates to also having immense humor. You can then likely gather that this is how they view circumstances in the practical based Earthly world. They see most of what goes on in a humor filled light rather than the tragic offended manner that many on Earth view circumstances around them in.

Many people sometimes feel as if the Divine does not love them, or that they're being ignored, neither of which are true. All are loved and no one is ignored. When it feels that way, then that has to do with your feelings, which ebb and flow. Feelings are not incessantly accurate when it's a reaction generated by the ego. The best way to feel loved by the Divine varies from one person to the next, but you can start by increasing your faith, having regular prayer, and conversations with the Divine, even if it feels like you're talking to no one. You are heard and eventually you start noticing the signs that you're not alone and that you are loved. In the physical world, the ego requires physical concrete material evidence of that love, but the love is felt from within like a great big warm hug.

Every soul has clairs (clear psychic senses) and chakras (soul energy points) that move up and down, and expand in and out. It acts like a gauge depending on where that soul's consciousness is at and what kind of emotions that soul is experiencing at any given moment during its existence. If you are riding sky high on love and joy, then your vibration raises. When your vibration rises, then so does your psychic antennae. If you are in the throes of any negative emotion, including complaining or whining about someone else, or what's being done to you, or how something upsets you, then this drops your vibration, and lowers your psychic frequency. It's just the way the soul is designed vibrating with varying colors and shades of the rainbow. It can glow a vibrant green color as it experiences healing, to an uplifting joyful bright yellow, to a purifying white, and then to the darkest shade of toxic black. This is all in the span of an hour depending on what that soul is experiencing in its life. If their emotions and moods fluctuate, then so does the psychic antennae.

Your soul at its core is a high vibrational being filled with ever flowing love, joy, and serenity. Don't forget who you are. Don't get lost in the negative toxic energy of the physical world. Take care of yourself, which means taking care of your soul and body on all levels as much as possible. Incorporate healthy life changes you can make today that will help you in awakening the parts of you that existed from the conception of your soul. These are the parts that can help you be happier, stronger, and that much more powerful.

You were born a vessel of love. Even if you do nothing with the gifts that exist within you, you will at least be shining that bright light of high vibrational energy onto all those in your path, which in turn tempers the severity of the bullets firing all over the place by the darkness of ego. The ego may have tantrums and cause all sorts of noise, but contrary to belief, love is more powerful than any other energy that exists on any plane in the end. Let your love flow and shine outwardly wherever you go. Revert to love, joy, and peace when possible. Take regular action steps that can help bring you back to this natural state of being whenever you falter on your path. Be conscious of who you are and the reservoir of gifts moving through you. This world needs more love and light in it. It is up to you to help guide others in that direction by doing the individual work to evolve and raise your consciousness. The planet doesn't need a ruler, since change starts with each individual shining this radiant love internally and outwardly.

CHAPTER THIRTEEN

Love Yourself Back to Life

You were born psychic and in tune to all that is beyond the physical world. This is the natural state of your soul. You were also born operating with highest vibrational qualities imaginable. All of this begins to fade in varying degrees due to human tampering and distractions during adolescence and your early human developmental years. These surroundings contain your caregivers, peers, the media you watch, and the community you reside in. All of this influences you on how to think, and what to follow, or what to believe in.

Having confidence in YOU is having confidence in God. The best parts of you are what

God is. He is not a man with a beard sitting high up on a throne looking for ways to judge you. The ego and the Darkness are what judge others negatively. God is made up of energy that has the highest vibration traits imaginable. Because His vibration is so high to the point that it's not comprehensible, this makes it difficult for human souls to reach Him. You cannot reach him when exuding any measure of negative emotion. As you dissolve negative feelings and thoughts at any given moment, then that's when your soul's vibration begins to lift up and raise into love where your psychic abilities grow stronger.

Others have been turning their backs on any mention of the word God because of the stigma that misguided souls have preached. They insist that God disapproves of you, which could not be further from the truth. His immense love for you is unconditional. He only expects that you put in an effort to be a better more loving and compassionate person. Evolve your soul in order to move onto brighter destinies. This isn't any different than what a good parent desires for their child.

The Earth plane is a school for souls that take on the roles of student or teacher. The teacher souls vacillate between the role of student and teacher because they are evolved enough to understand that soul growth and learning will never cease to exist. The student souls are what we call Baby Souls because they are newborn souls that sparked out of God and immediately incarnated into an Earthly life to begin their first life run in soul school. They are easy to spot because they tend to be more naïve and innocent, yet some of them are filled with hate and destruction because they have not gone through enough soul training to be able to master the ego. The ego became this way due to how they were raised in their human environment. Hate and negativity are passed down into the human child. When you train your child early on to have love and compassion for all souls, then they will grow up this way evolving rather quickly. In that respect, the child's particular parent has the important mission and purpose of raising their child's soul consciousness. Teacher souls have an ego as well since all souls on Earth have an ego, but the teacher souls are a bit more advanced in that they are instantly cognizant of when they are going too far when it comes to ego.

Some souls are experiencing a repeat life in order to continue their soul's education so they can continue to expand and evolve into more love. They cannot move on to new destinies until individual soul lessons are learned, gained, and accepted.

God loves all souls more than can be comprehended. This includes even the most distasteful human being is equally loved. It is the same way a parent who has several children that are each different, but all loved equally.

Your soul is awesomely wonderful and loved by God and the universe beyond measure and comprehension. How awesome is that to be loved no matter how you're feeling? All human souls desire to be loved and will seek it out in friendships, family members, colleagues and lovers. This is with the hope that these other souls will give you that all-encompassing love. The love exists within you to begin with and can be conjured up naturally by doing the work to revert to love whenever possible.

When you are experiencing a block, then this could be a sign that the soul is starving for stimulation and creativity. Express yourself artistically without censure or fear that others will not approve or like what you do. Allow the vibrating power of spirit to flow through and awaken the creative part of you. Take care of yourself on all levels inside and out. This will assist in giving you greater energy, stamina, and focus, not to mention a stronger connection with your Spirit team.

Having a crystal-clear communication line with God will enable you to make sounder decisions in your life. It will assist you in reaching a higher vibration state than if you didn't have that connection. Creativity helps in raising your vibration into high feelings of joy, love, and peace, while boosting your faith and optimism. Diving into creative projects or obtaining a creative slant in your nature and day to day dealings also help in lifting blocks in your way to love. When you are enjoying your life, then it shows, and this is a powerful attractor for good things including a potential love partner.

Awakening the creative spirit in you is also unleashing that part of you that is connected to God. The creative part of you within that is in tune to all nuances in and around you. It is your inner child that is full of love, joy, and peace around the clock. This is why detoxing and watching what you ingest are important. It is because these all play a factor into what drains your life force energy zapping any ounce of creativity in you. Take care of all parts of you. Watch what you ingest and the energy of the thoughts you put into your mind.

Self-care is a not only a luxury, but a necessity. Love all that you are, and remember to pat yourself on the back for any job well done. When you've accomplished anything at all, then treat yourself to something good in celebration. Whether that's a hiking sabbatical trip or that t-shirt or music album you always wanted. Go for it! Reward yourself. You deserve the endless reservoirs of success and prosperity in all areas of your life that exist. Never stop being creative and live your life from the heart. Create out of love and give out of love.

I've always felt alive diving into artistic endeavors and in unleashing my creative spirit. When I was moody, depressed, or angry, I'd find something creative to do that dissolved those blocks and lift me back into the higher dominions of joy and optimism. Escaping into a creative world is where I've always been happiest. The world is a tragic place thanks to the darkness of ego in humankind, but in the creative world is where all love and pure enjoyment exist.

The same way your life force is ignited is the same way that your creative spirit is unleashed. It's a lifestyle change you adopt by changing your attitude, feelings, and thoughts to that of optimism. It's finding a love and passion for something and diving into it. This is getting back into the joy of your life, which is an inspiration in itself. It is the beginning stages of pulling that tiny spark out of you that grows dim due to life circumstances. Light a match on this ember and allow it to inflame into creation. Escape into the magnificent worlds your mind daydreams and visualizes. Find something creative you enjoy doing and master it. Immerse your whole being into the revelations that come to you. Apply it to your daily life by coming up with new pioneering ways in excelling. This assists you in your soul's growth and raises your vibration to the place where the connection with Heaven is made. You are creatively powerful! Activate, awaken, and ignite this part of you. Experience the exhilarating love high that comes with creativity.

When you love and enjoy what you're doing, then you're infusing this love enjoyment energy into your work. This is a positive ingredient that will attract a like-minded energy to it. If you do your work with fear and worry, then you will attract that kind of negative energy to it. The energy will be a block that prevents love success from entering the picture. Stay positive, optimistic, and joyful with all that you do when you can help it.

Diving into creativity is a great way to shake yourself out of any funk you experience. It helps you navigate through the treacherous waters of human life. It assists you in finding innovative ways to solutions, which can carry over to other aspects of your life from the business arena to love relationships. It helps you to think outside of the box and showcase your originality because everything you're doing while being creative is solely you. It pulls out the deepest parts of your soul. A photographer is being creative by taking pictures. They might spend hours taking a variety of photos of different flowers in a garden. By doing this they see the beauty and love around them. These creative gifts come out of you and mirror what you have within. Your true nature is revealed back to you as a result.

Creativity is a great reminder of who your soul truly is. Diving into creative and artistic pursuits brings this love out of you. Creativity cures boredom or lulls in your day while helping you to express yourself in positive ways. It gets your energy moving to see things in a different way. When human souls are bored, they tend to reach for an addiction. They might log online, surf the Internet pointlessly, visit a social media site, or log on to a phone app for human contact and stimulation that ceases to exist in their physical reality. You feel even more lonely and bored after hours of being unproductive with that. This becomes a bigger problem when you discover that this is how you spend every second of your day. If you didn't have that one step to check your social media page throughout the day, then you fear you might lose out on life.

Diving into artistic pursuits helps awaken your inner child. Your inner child is the person you were before age ten. It is the innocent all loving part of you as a child that had no judgment or criticisms of other people. Those criticisms came upon you through your environment and at the hands of those who heavily influenced you. If you grew up at the hands of bullying or any form of abuse, then this has a detrimental effect on your inner child. If you grew up in a community where the people were prejudice or racist, then the chances of you developing this racism trait are higher than anyone else.

You were not born racist and nor were you prejudice against anyone and their life choices. This goes for any sort of bias from political affiliations, religion, or hatred of someone's sexual orientation. None of that exists with your inner child. Your inner child is the part of you that has the most access to God, because it is all love, joy, and peace. Your inner child is the one who knows how to have fun and can see the innocence in people without criticism. It is jaded adults that did not evolve that spend their days attacking and judging others.

The inner child has no interest in lower energy behavior. It doesn't even cross its mind. Your inner child longs for release and fun if only your ego would pull that part of you back out to play again. When the dark ego dominates and grows lost in the physical world, your inner child screams for attention and love. Diving into creative artistic pursuits is a great way to fire up your inner child. When your inner child remains buried under rubble, then feelings of emptiness and loss begin to rise. Some go through these feelings of being lost during pinnacle times in their life. It can be brought upon due to a loss of any kind, such as the loss of a job, a friendship, a lover, or any other loss to something that gave you a sense of security or happiness.

Your inner child is who you were before all of the layers of trauma and life experiences jaded you. It was when you saw life without judgment or critique. You saw life through the lens of joy and love. It was before human tampering made you despise anyone different from you. Those who despise someone that is different we're not that way when they were four years old. It was their caregivers, peers, community, and society influence that taught all of that stuff. If God raised you, then you would've grown up to see the love in all souls. You would exude love and joy full time. When you were born, you were immensely psychic, and filled with overflowing feelings of love, joy, and peace. You were wide eyed ready to absorb everything around you. You saw the beauty in life, in the colors, and in the trees. You were also a sponge absorbing the environment you were growing up in.

Hug More!

Hugging and touching have immense healing properties to the soul. It awakens your inner child, which is also connected to the creative part of you. Are you overworked, stressed, depressed, or angry? Hug others more and allow them to hug you. Hugging lowers your blood pressure, relieves stress, and releases the brain chemical Oxytocin. This contributes to positive bonding or otherwise known as the love hormone. Hugging reminds you that we're all on the same side. Many of the cure all remedies for so many issues reside within you. Hugs are one of the various activities that promote positive health. And hugs don't cost anything. They're free!

If you're willing to part with a hug, then do it more often. Hug your friend, your lover, and even your pet! Animals are souls and crave the hug of another. Hugging is one of the many great vibration enhancers. For a brief moment your soul can breathe while in the midst of a hug. It tears away any off-putting ions that latch itself onto the aura around your spirit. You experience release and you understand what freedom feels like.

Everyone needs a hug whether they like to admit it or not. The most toughened human soul needs that love to tear down the walls they've built around their heart. You've likely come across someone who you try to hug, and they clam up or turn into a brick wall barely giving back the hug. They're terribly uncomfortable being touched, as it's not something they likely grew up getting enough of. They hardened over time at some point in their life.

Many are angry, depressed, or feeling any other kind of emotion that disconnects your soul from a feeling of joy, peace, or love. Those qualities are traits, which are innate inside of you, but buried so far deep it can't climb out of the hole it's trapped itself in. The world needs a war on hugs. If you're going to complain about something, then complain that you're receiving too much love, hugs, and kisses from the world. There are millions of nerve endings in the human skin and to experience touch activates these nerves prompting you to raise your vibration.

Unleash Your Inner Joy!

Joy is one of the highest vibrating energies that exist next to love. When someone laughs into hysterics, you sense the infectious energy. Suddenly strangers around that person light up with a smile. Someone else's energy will affect others around them. If they're being negative, then that will transfer. If they're infectiously giggly, then that will transfer. Seeing the fun and lightheartedness in situations raises your vibration. It lightens the heavy loaded burdens of stress.

When your vibration is high, you attract in brighter circumstances to you. If you're stuck in negative feelings, then call upon your Spirit team and ask them to help in elevating your soul into a happier space. Request that they guide you to getting back into the joy of your life again. Radiating with joy is what brings more of that good stuff to you. No one wants to be around a miserable stressed out and depressed grump. Feeling joy while visualizing your desires is what helps the manifestation process take place more quickly too. If everyone exuded their soul's natural state, then there would be peace on Earth. Everyone would be happy because no one is treating others disrespectfully or clawing their way to achieve or dominate. If everyone paid attention to their Spirit team, then love would reign. Archangel Jophiel is the hierarchy angel to call on to bring more joy and beauty into your life.

The Heart Chakra

The Heart Chakra is the fourth chakra energy center part of your soul. It is located in your physical heart and chest area. It is also in the middle of the eight core chakras blending both the physical and emotional/spiritual parts of you. It spins more rapidly than the previous three chakras illuminating a beautiful emerald green light.

As you might likely guess, the Heart Chakra is connected to all things having to do with love. This includes your love relationships and connections with others including friendships, family members, and colleagues. If these connections are toxic or cause you ill will feelings then this breaks your Heart Chakra.

An ex-lover has pulled a number on you leaving you saddened and moving through all of the various states of emotion from depression to anger to revenge. While this is a natural reaction to having a love relationship end, it also muddies up your Heart Chakra. This blocks love from coming in.

The Heart Chakra is connected to issues with all relationships from love, personal, business, to your negative states of emotion. When you cut off love and do not allow love in for fear of getting hurt or any other reason, then you clog up the

Heart Chakra.

Ways to clean and clear the Heart Chakra is to remember to get back to that place where you can love again. When you forgive a partner, you begin the process of cleaning the Heart Chakra. Perhaps they cheated on you or were abusive. Both of which are difficult to forgive or forget. Regardless, in order to clear the Heart Chakra, you must reach that place where you forgive them for yourself and for your own benefit.

You can mentally say, "What you did to me was not cool, but I forgive you so that I don't have to carry this pain anymore. And now I release you from my aura permanently."

The Heart Chakra is also connected to your Clairsentience psychic clair sense. Having a strong Heart Chakra awakens your Clairsentience. This is your psychic feeling sense. Activate your Heart Chakra by lifting your emotions and feelings to that of love, joy, and peace. This will bring on a crystal-clear communication line with Heaven through your Clairsentience. Visualize healing green light shining onto it blasting away any and all negative toxic debris, and then exhale that burden out of you.

Those with a strong Heart Chakra are warm, friendly, and open. They hold no judgment or criticism. You can likely guess that all of those people that post negative words, attacks, and comments online have a muddied down Heart Chakra.

Other ways to awaken your Heart Chakra are through having a healthy loving relationship or by expressing kind words to those around you. Being supportive, loving, and partaking in self-care activates this chakra. Do things that give you a euphoric happy feeling of love including watching a romantic comedy. Love all that you are inside and out. Love is the reason all are here and this is why having a beautiful radiating Heart Chakra is especially vital to your overall health and well-being.

Archangel Raphael, Archangel Jophiel, Archangel Haniel, or Archangel Chamuel are the hierarchy angels to call on to assist you with your Heart Chakra. They work with you on matters of love, healing, emotions, and attracting in high vibration connections.

CHAPTER FOURTEEN

Bring Out the Good Vibrations

Show your best self by becoming a fearless confident soul that walks in faith. Share your love light with others whenever you can. Let it out and let it shine bright. Visualize yourself surrounded by a massive pink rose light that vibrates with white sparkles as you move about this creation. This inspires a mighty movement of love and peace. The hardness and toxicity that has plagued humankind for so long is outdated. The light of love exists inside of you. You must allow it to take back the control of your surroundings and burst on out of you. Be a warrior of light by doing your best to stay in that space even when you stumble upon a roadblock or a difficult human soul. Demanding people are merely acting out from their ego, which has no power or validity with anything real or long lasting.

The ego lives in fear and acts out in fits of temper much like a child having an outburst when it doesn't get what it wants. You find peace, joy, strength and love when you remain centered in the light. When you lose your way, ask for heavenly assistance to get back on track. The more you ask for help and work with your Spirit team to reach this space of contentment, then the easier it gets.

What can work for you to bring in your Spirit team might be lighting a candle and meditating on this light. Call in your Spirit team to begin the process of re-aligning your soul. Empty out your negative thoughts as you focus on this candlelight. Close your eyes and envision that the flame of the light is taking over any negative thoughts and blasting it away while lifting it off your body. Make room in your consciousness to receive the messages coming in from Spirit to help you be at peace and feel encompassed by love. You can call on them any time, day, or night. There is no special invocation that needs to happen. You can mentally communicate with them while you're brushing your teeth, taking a shower, getting dressed, and walking to your car. The more you do it, the more you'll find the most effective way that works for you.

I have crossed paths with a wide variety of people who have different belief systems and values. I have witnessed those who might disagree with any of this or who find it to be ineffective, yet these are the same people that struggle in a constant uphill battle in life. Or they might be the ones who have been stagnant with no hope for escape. When in those states, your ego dominates your life big time ensuring that you never progress.

Within you is the knowledge of all soul lifetimes you've endured. Within you is the knowledge of why you are here. Pay attention to your intuition as that is one of the many barometer gauges that exist within your soul that accurately receives heavenly messages. All human souls receive heavenly communication every day without exception. It is irrelevant what the soul's personal values and beliefs are, and whether they're aware that it is indeed their Guides and Angels. Pay attention to the messages in order to help you navigate through life much easier than if you were not aware of them.

Keeping your vibration high takes daily work. It's a lifestyle and view change you're adopting. One day you are riding on cloud nine with joy, which raises your vibration. Your vibration remains high until a negative thought enters your mind thus causing it to take a dip again. The next day you go on a drinking binge. This drinking binge prompts your vibration to drop astronomically. It can be a struggle to raise it in the Earth's dense filled plane than it is to drop it. Raising it back up can feel like pushing a huge boulder up a steep hill. Those privy to this knowledge can raise their vibration much easier than someone unaware of what to do in order to get it there. Having an interfering culprit like the ego is what gets its kicks out of double-crossing you and ensuring your vibration stays low. It makes sure that you do not succeed. When you make a commitment to incorporating higher vibration methods into your life every day, then you will notice the changes in your life shifting in a more positive direction.

It's easy to lose sight of why you're here. The way human life has been set up and structured by the ego in others has caused enormous discontent. Human ego trained other souls to be unhappy and glum by thriving for nonsense. Not everyone is affected by the harsh energies of the planet. These people have made adjustments to their lifestyle choices. This includes living in areas of nature with little to no chaos and people. Watching what they ingest in their physical bodies and taking care of it through daily exercise. They ensure the people they surround themselves with are high vibrational. They avoid the negativities of social media, the internet and gossip entertainment.

There are a great many positives to Earthly life. Human souls took what they innately learned from the spirit world and built homes, created work and jobs for others, designed transportation, as well as an ease of communication through advanced technological devices. These are some of the fantastic concrete necessities for human life. These are practical ways of surviving on a planet that is spilling over the edges.

However, interpersonal relationships continue to suffer sliding rapidly on a decline. Love is lacking in others while cruelty and unfriendliness is gaining steam. It is true that human souls manage to find the love when a crisis hit. They intervene when they notice someone is being pushed down, but the love they exude in those instances is temporary. You grow lost in the nonsense of the noise of the ego. Some are consumed by jobs they're not happy in, or you're living check-to-check, or struggling to find work. Perhaps you're in relationships that are unsatisfying or you're perpetually single longing for a long-term committed love relationship that never surfaces. You're forced to be in situations you do not want to be in. What an effort it is to get to a place of feeling eternally happy.

When you're faced with circumstances that do not jive with your higher self, examine how you arrived at that place. Look at the underlying cause that has prompted you to feel negative when this happens. Identify it and then dig deep into understanding why it has upset you.

There are circumstances that no doubt have made you angry or prompted feelings of discomfort. Maybe you ran into someone at the store who was rude to you. You being a sensitive absorbed that like nobody's business. It ends up putting you in a funk for the rest of the day. For some sensitive's, they'll be angry for a minute, others for hours, or you could be one of those who immerses in the energy for the rest of the day. Avoid beating yourself up over it. It just means that you're a hypersensitive psychic sponge. You have compassion and love within you as all souls do, even though this might be difficult to grasp.

Whenever you witness ugliness in someone else, remember that they were born with the deepest love and compassion beyond measure. What you're observing with them is the darkness of ego at its worst. This soul has given its power away to the Darkness, their lower self, and ego. The ego cannot be reasoned with or convinced of anything, but of what it wants. The ego seeks to sabotage themselves or others. A high vibrational soul who is not pleased with something does not waste its time resorting to negativity or in giving it any attention. It only focuses on what it enjoys.

When you witness aggression or disrespectful behavior flying at you, then you will absorb that energy. It seeps into your aura and soul. It causes an array of negative circumstances and moods to assault you. What is important is that you find positive exercises that can assist you in releasing it and letting that go. It might feel easier said than done, but when a slight happens in your world, your ego has trouble letting go of it. When you understand this concept of separating yourself from the troublesome ego, it becomes simpler to manage and temper it.

When you have a higher degree of sensitivity than other souls, then you are more likely to be affected by someone else's ego. You're a psychic sponge who easily absorbs the negative or off-putting energies in others. It is a gift, but at times it can feel like a curse when you enter environments with human souls displaying low vibrational behavioral patterns. You absorb that negative energy which drops your mood affecting your inner and outer world.

When you grow negative, moody, or agitated, then this is a sign of two possible conclusions. One is that you've ingested low vibrational foods or drinks. Or you may have absorbed this energy from someone toxic you crossed paths with. It can be a stranger on the sidewalk who walked past you. If they're displaying low vibrational behavior, then that energy is lodged in their aura. As a tuned in sensitive psychic sponge, you've absorbed that into your aura sometimes without knowing it. Although, the super tuned in psychic sponges are typically aware they just absorbed this energy from someone in passing.

The souls you absorbed this energy from do not always intend to have a low vibration. It's usually done innocently and naively, or sometimes they do not know any better. Some souls have not evolved enough to be more in tune to something outside of themselves. This is partially why that particular soul is living an Earthly life.

Those that are psychically in tune beyond the physical are turned off by harsh people and energies. They steer clear of those that perpetually display low vibrational traits. It can be your employer or someone you work with who puts on the fakeness whenever you enter the room. As a tuned in soul, you can sense them a mile away. They're threatened by your higher frequency energy. They subconsciously know that you're on to them. This also turns off a lower vibrational energy in someone else. Low vibrational human souls are threatened by someone that exudes a high vibrational energy. The low vibrational soul's ego feels out of your league. High vibrational people don't feel threatened by others, but instead repel the lower energies.

This coldness and reserve have grown in others thanks to the technological age. Newer and future generations are being raised on devices that train you to be lacking in honest face-to-face soul connections. For those that have gone out on a date, you've probably noticed some of the typical preliminary questions. They want to know what your job is or what kind of work do you do. What kind of car do you drive? These ego driven questions are externally based. Your job does not define you in real reality, but the human ego has set their life up in a way that their whole world revolves around what kind of job you do. Who cares what you do for a living or what you have in your possession. Unless you're working in a field that is your passion and it brings you joy, then it is irrelevant what kind of work you do. This passion is your life purpose, but many do not work in jobs that are their passion. For most, it is a paycheck that squeezes the life force out of that soul. They're usually under stress and grumbling about life in general.

When you absorb the ions of negative and cold energy around you, then this can put a damper on your spirit until you address it. You can sit around and hope that something amazing will happen around you that will suddenly raise your vibration, or you can address it and do something about it immediately. It can be going for a walk in a nature setting. This is followed by taking deep healthy breaths in while requesting that your spirit team release any and all negative energy that has latched onto your soul. It can be getting together with an optimistic friend who observes healthy life choices, or someone who always lifts your aura just by being in your vicinity. You can throw on a funny movie or make love to your relationship partner. What you're trying to do is re-raise your vibration. Taking basic soul enhancing steps when an assault has attacked your aura can do the trick.

Everyone has experienced some hard times at one time or another. You have negative things to say about it. The ego fixates on the horrid that came out of that. Rise above your ego and ask yourself, "What greatness did I get out of that experience? What was awesome about it?"

The soul's experiences happen for a reason regardless if they're challenging or not. It is not because you did something to deserve it, but because your soul is destined for greatness. You're here in this Earthly life school to find ways that suit you in order to enhance your soul and spirit. You're not here to find out the latest sale on jeans or rip through relationships selfishly with no care in the world. In order to improve, you have much to gain. When something negative happens in your world, work on looking at it from an optimistic perspective.

An exercise you can do is to pick up a journal or a notebook. Use that notepad as your diary to put in only optimistic viewpoints in your life. When you find that you're buried heavily in negative thoughts and emotions unable to break away, take a moment to pull the notebook out. Devote a page or more to whatever it is that is upsetting you. If it's a person you know, then write that person's name in your journal entry. Instead of focusing on what they did to upset you or whatever circumstance has upset you, shift that into something positive. Think about all of the qualities you love about the person that has angered you. Remove your ego from the equation and look at that person through the eyes of an egoless angel. List everything that is positive about them and how that affects you in an optimistic way.

When someone has hurt or angered you, of course it's going to be difficult to see them through the eyes of love. Know that when you're looking at them through the eyes of love, you're not condoning their behavior, and nor do you have to remain best friends with them. You're doing this exercise as a release. It's for your benefit in order to remove that old, tired, angry energy you're carrying around that surrounds the person or circumstance. You do not need that energy, but in order to release it, acknowledging it with love is what raises your vibration. When your vibration is raised you are more apt to receiving clearer communication from the spirit world, which in turn assists you on your path towards abundance in all forms.

Your mind may begin to wander to all of the things you feel this person has done that has hurt or upset you. However, you will not write those things down. Remember this is a positive journal. You will immediately adjust your thoughts back to the positive things about this person. Let's say it was an ex-lover who cheated on you, was abusive, or left you and the relationship. You will not write any of those things down, but rather will focus on their good qualities. If you're only able to come up with one good quality, then write that one down. It is an exercise that takes much effort in this case, because you're holding anger towards this person for doing one or all of the things I suggested. Your ego refuses to see the goodness in someone who has upset or hurt you.

If it is a circumstance that happened to cause you upset, then you will write down in this journal the optimistic features that have come out of that. For example, you receive a traffic ticket. Instead of focusing heavily on how you have no time to take care of the ticket, or no money to pay for it, write down the positive benefits that you've gained from the ticket. You might write something down like: "This has taught me to drive more carefully."

That statement feels far better than saying, "I have no money. How am I going to pay for this! It wasn't even my fault!"

This exercise may not immediately change your life, but it will gradually guide you into positively changing your life. It will assist you in getting into the habit of bouncing back from upsetting situations much more quickly. It will help you to view circumstances and people in a more positive light as well as re-training your mind to think in a different way. The key is if you're going to play this game, then you have to play objectively. Putting all things positive and optimistic in this journal is the exercise. Only write your blessings, appreciations and gratitude for situations and people in your life.

This absolutely includes everything and everyone that causes you to feel negative emotions. This might be challenging, but in the end it will be rewarding as you are re-training your mind to think positively. This raises your vibration in the process, which assists with attracting in positive circumstances and people to you over the course of time. Because it raises your vibration, it also clears out the debris that accumulates in and around the communication line to Heaven and your Spirit team. If it doesn't do anything, but allow you to start shining your true loving light, then that is all that matters in the end.

The ego is a wretched problem seeker. It might appear to be louder than your higher self and your Spirit team of guides and angels. This is due to a couple of factors. The atmosphere of the Earth plane is extremely thick and dense that connecting to the Other Side through all of the toxic debris makes it challenging. Your guides and angels are louder and more powerful than any ego. Yet, when the soul is in the Earth dimension, the communication lines are heavier and dirtier. The ego rises through the dirt. It already rises as soon as your soul enters into this human life. The ego is activated in a big way. When the soul is in the earth plane it's like roaming through life with ear plugs on. Anyone who has put ear plugs on to sleep at night may point out how they can sometimes faintly hear light sounds with them on. The higher self strains to hear Heaven through this muffled sound. When a human soul lives in a higher vibrational state, this allows light in, which gives rise to the higher self. Suddenly that soul is hearing their guides and angels more clearly than usual.

You are not alone as you are surrounded by at least one Spirit Guide and one Guardian Angel from your human birth until human death. They assist you down the right path in order to fulfill your purpose while here. When you are in your higher self's state you connect with your Spirit team on the Other Side with greater efficiency. When you are in your lower self's state or ego, then you block heavenly guidance and messages that keep you on the right path and assist you in achieving your desires. In my connections with Heaven, I've discovered that all are loved and seen through the eyes of love. Do your best to keep the darkness of your ego in check and exude love full time!

Abundance Profusion Exercise

The following is an abundance visualization exercise that you may choose to do to help train your mind to welcome in blessings in any form, whether that's love, career, finances, or stronger health. You may also choose to expand on it and create your own exercise that works for you.

Find a comfortable undisturbed space to lie down on the floor or in a nature setting, such as a patch of grass in a park or your backyard. If you're in a room, then look up at the ceiling. If you're outside then look up at the sky, pending the sun is not in your eye line.

Imagine the sky or your ceiling opening up letting bright Heavenly Divine light in. It breaks through blasting away all negativity and debris in your midst. Now visualize the sky or ceiling cracking open even more. Visualize infinite money bills falling out of it and on top of you while you lay there. You can create an ambiance of candles and listen to some good music as you lay there with a smile visualizing all these riches falling on you from above. These riches also equate to feelings of a strong powerful positive well-being, good friends, great health, lovely home, and a beautiful radiant love partner that you match with the same veracity. You can substitute the money for other desires. If it's love you long for, then visualize red roses dropping down on you.

Think about the roadblocks that constantly get in your way of attracting the blessings you wish would transpire. It can be your own thoughts and feelings or another person. As you think about each roadblock that stops the flow of positive abundance, begin putting into practice a visualization exercise. This is one where you close your eyes and imagine those blocks being blasted away with white light. This allows the block to disintegrate and fall away from you to reveal what you've long desired. Imagine each of these roadblocks dissolving away out of your aura.

Remove all mental obstacles of lack and begin to visualize what you want. For example, if you want a house, then visualize this house and the surrounding area of what you would like it to be.

What kind of house is it? What does it look like in your imagination?

Visualize yourself walking through the front door of this house and moving through it. Who is in this house with you? Is it a love interest? A man or a woman? What are they like? Are there other people there or is it just you? Imagine this desire as if it's happening and has come true now. Surround yourself and your thoughts with this image in your mind. What you visualize and envision you eventually receive. Through the power of your thoughts and feeling energy, you are bending towards that dream coming true. Do this regularly until the dream has become a reality no matter how long it takes.

The human ego mind sees things as fear based and riddled with negative emotions such as anxiety or depression. The higher self soul sees the potential and capabilities of achieving abundance. Allow abundance to come crashing into your life with welcome open arms.

Tell yourself daily that you are worthy of receiving abundance. You are qualified, worthy, and deserving of good. You are filled up with a never-ending overflowing cornucopia of abundance. The floodgates have opened and the door to abundance has slammed open. Light is soaring in with abundant energy all throughout it. This light surrounds you like a great big hug. Abundance is all that it entails from a wonderful relationship, magnificent health, good friendships, etc. It can be feeling abundant spiritually and emotionally.

Move into the alignment that you believe you have everything you could possibly want in your life. See it as if it's live and in motion now even if it hasn't transpired yet. Allow your mind to see that it is. Allow your feelings to sense the great feelings associated with how you would feel to have that life. See and feel it as if it is here with you in your mind now. What will your state of being feel like?

Find that optimistic uplifting space knowing you have all that you could ever want and more. Get your energy into this positive alignment with God now. It surrounds you in a magnetic powerful way that you can feel it as you move about through life. You feel God's magnificent presence working with you to keep this momentum going. You are a powerful magical manifester with the ability to create all that you desire by the actions and energy of your thoughts and feelings. This is your winning card in attracting in blessings. You have these skills within you. Start taking action steps towards attracting what you desire today.

CHAPTER FIFTEEN

Universal Spiritual Love

All souls incarnate on Earth for the purpose of love, whether that is to learn to love, to teach love, to express love, or all of the above. As you've probably noticed, many people haven't been able to master the basic art of love. This includes the ones that protest that they love everybody. Attacking people over a statement that messed with your delicate sensitivities is not love.

Be like the egoless angels, filled with an all-consuming love and forgiveness shining God's rays of light down onto all those void of love and in great need of healing and clarity. In their eyes, you are loved without judgment. It is the darkness of human ego that harshly judges others. This doesn't mean that someone committing cruel crimes on someone else will receive a free pass of forgiveness, but in Heaven's eyes you are expected to correct poor choices. You are expected to ask for forgiveness and to correct any wrongs you've been enacting on someone else. This is part of developing a deeper evolving consciousness. Partaking in wrongdoing knowing you'll be forgiven doesn't count, since that deceptiveness is taken into consideration. It's like giving someone a gift with the hopes of getting something in return. This isn't authentic giving when you desire something back.

All human souls have an ego with varying shades of light and dark. It's the darkness of ego that causes the most unnecessary chaos. It prompts others to antagonize, attack, criticize, judge, hate, and all the cousins of those words. The world in general is loveless. This is primarily witnessed and absorbed on a massive scale all over the media. Comments posted are filled with bickering, attacking, confronting, and disagreeing with hostility and negativity. It's all noise that does nothing to positively serve, assist, or change anything. None of that is helpful and nor does it convince someone who disagrees with one's argument. All it does is breed negativity, which is absorbed by others and then passed around to one another like poison seeping into your soul.

If this is what the current general population of humanity is like, then it's no wonder there are many struggling to find love in any form. Being in that space does not attract in love. There is no room for someone else's opinion or choices that differ from your own to begin with. Having a warm inviting openness is what attracts in positive love circumstances to you. You start within you and then work your way out. You change the way you view circumstances and project that outwardly. You accept others for their differences, values, and choices even if you personally or morally disagree.

You can stay stuck in a negative mindset and despise other people, but the only person it hurts in the end is you. This negative energy weighs down your soul and stalls it from evolving movement, because it's dead set on holding a grudge. There is no clarity when the ego is running the show. At the end of your life run, the truth becomes clear as you are shown images of all your human years on the planet and what you did or did not do with it. You're shown what you said or did not say to someone. This includes how that affected you and the other person, whether it was a loved one, or an acquaintance, or stranger. You experience those emotions through all perceptions. It would be more beneficial to grow more aware today through psychoanalysis work.

There was a time when physical violence reigned supreme, and while it still exists, the new violence that rules is through words, thoughts, and feelings. This is how the Darkness does its work. The Darkness knows this energy moves rapidly able to bring out the most heinous ego imaginable out of the once purest Light. His goal is to bring everyone down as quickly as possible. He's been successful at it for so many centuries. Become the example of love, goodness, respect, and light. This is what always wins in the end.

You were born a pure Light of love, peace, joy, compassion, and understanding. You were filled with immense passion and love for all you came across. Throughout the soul's journey on Earth, it is faced with temptations, judgments, and harm by those around it who function primarily from the darkness of ego. It is your job to remember who you are and who you were when you were born out of God's love. It is one of your purposes and missions to rise above the hatred, darkness, and lower energies that assault you everyday, and move back into being the centered Light that you were made in.

Pay attention to the moments when you find you've become guilty of being a toxic monster and climb out of that painful abyss as quickly as possible. Extricate the cause that triggered you to fall for the dark one's deception. Kick it out of your life for good. Don't forget who you are. You were born perfect in His love's Light. You have the power at your fingertips to create the most splendid magnificent life by the vibration energy of your thoughts.

Every soul on the planet experiences fear throughout their Earthly life. It is the one common trait that everyone has listed in their soul contract before incarnating into an Earthly life. You're a feeling, breathing, thinking consciousness moving about in a physical vessel for a variety of reasons. Every single person on the planet has a reason for being here, even if you have no clue what it is at any given moment. It is up to you to discover your numerous purposes that are connected to one singular intention. There are the default motives that all are here such as learning to love, but there are other goals outside of that even though love is always at the top of the list in the end.

Fear stalls humanity from evolving as witnessed in the centuries of evolution on the planet. While progress continues to be made in diminutive trickles, improvement still moves at a glacial rate thanks to humanities fear. It should not take hundreds of years to advance in the tiniest steps despite taking what we can get. This is due to individual fear resisting against changing their perception and awakening their consciousness to that of love. Finding the space of love and respect is challenging for the mediocre mind. Training every breathing organism to snap out of it takes an army of lights to do their part. Extricate fear from your aura and become unstoppable.

Move out of fear and toxicity, and close your eyes, take a deep breath in and feel and experience His love light moving into and through you allowing it to become one with you. You have a centered Light within you that is waiting and willing to be ignited whenever you allow it. Make that choice to become one with it. You have arrived in God's economy when you become a love blessing to others. You are simultaneously becoming a blessing to yourself as well too.

When your vibration is low, you feel and experience negative feelings such as anger, depression, stress, irritability, and so on. When your vibration is high, you feel euphoric feelings of joy, love, peace, and contentment.

A vibration in spiritual concepts is your overall emotional well-being and energetic state. Feelings such as depression, anger, and guilt lower your vibration, but if you're feeling joyful, in love, and centered, then your vibration begins to rise. The lowest vibrational state includes feelings of anger, stress, or depression. Watch out if you're experiencing a combination of all three at once.

The highest vibrational states are feelings of peace, joy, and love. Experiencing all three of those states at the same time makes you a high vibrational powerhouse! Love is the highest vibrational state possible, so always revert to raising your emotional state to that of love.

The lifelong battle with demons in my personal life is always matched with those from beyond the veil consistently pointing me towards the Light. When touched by the power, it is unconditional love experienced that no words can describe. The soul is overwhelmed in that radiance when enveloped in its arms. The answer to the question of the meaning of life is always the same. The answer is LOVE.

The more enlightened you become, and the more you raise your consciousness, then the better off you'll be. This doesn't mean that you'll be stress free, but you'll certainly experience less stress while being able to efficiently navigate through the treacherous waters of the practical world easier than if you did not have that raised consciousness.

Imagine if every human soul found the gift of love within them. No one would need to be here since that would be Utopia. When you find the space of love and learn to keep it there and revert to it when possible, then the closer you are to creating Heaven on Earth. It's a beautiful thing when one soul awakens another in a positive way just by being in their presence.

Deep down every soul longs to re-attain and achieve that blissful excellence that gives the impression of unabashed joy and serenity. It is a condition where unwavering love and harmony surround you in a protected cushion. Transcending beyond the dull insensible frustrated Earthy life and into the natural condition the soul once habited is a goal that delights. It reminds the soul of where it came from. You runaway and travel around the globe searching for a sign of this utopia, only to be consistently left with disappointment. This is because utopia begins and ends inside the spark that burns within your soul like a pilot light.

The spirit worlds are the ultimate Utopian paradise that is an unbelievable spectacle. It mirrors the nature settings and natural wonders on Earth, but is even more vibrant, lush, and magical than the human mind could comprehend. It would have to be because why would a place full of 100% uplifting joy, love, and peace be less than the physical Earthly plane? The Earthly plane is a school set up that house's spirits of every variety in a human body.

Human beings ruling their life from the darkness of ego cause the majority of misery experienced. If every single soul on the planet were in tune and connected with the Divine full time, while using their God given born traits of love, then Earth would be as blissful as Heaven.

Coming to the end of the road as you close your Earthly life chapter up, you realize if you hadn't before that it was always intended to be about love. Your soul was born from a source of love and you will die right back into that love. Love is the most powerful energy foundation that exists in all dimensions. The only thing that matters is love. The best way to channel energy positively is to remember all things connected to love. Love is what kills energy like anger, sadness, fear, and worry. Outstretch your arms, release any fears, and fall back into the arms of this love. Allow it to protect and guide you on your Earthly journey.

Bring your soul to that beautiful glorious space of centeredness, serenity, and peace. Ignore any drama swirling around you and view circumstances from an emotionally detached perspective without judgment. Increase your faith through prayer and regular conversations with the Divine, knowing and understanding that you are loved and watched over.

Every day should be the most magical time of the year, but the lack of love on the planet that continues to be prevalent makes it less enchanting. Remember to love and accept others even if their values are differing from yours. This is easier said than done since many have forgotten about the basic concept of what love is. Humanity continues to have a long way to go before every soul on the planet is aware that it's about love.

Treat everyone with kindness and compassion even if they don't share your values. This goes for all sides of the spectrum, as everyone becomes guilty of it at one time or another. It's not okay to treat others badly. It's not okay to abuse the luxuries you've been given as a free will thinking conscious soul being. It's one thing to defend yourself from someone who has accosted or randomly disrespected you, but it's another to take it upon yourself to harass someone because they're different and not a clone of you. You reach no middle ground when you're that rigid.

The ultimate reason all are here is to love and to learn how to love. You cannot learn that unless you're thrown onto a planet with others who are different from you. Learn to accept others and see someone's personal truth. You're not saying you agree with them, but a way shower illuminates the way by example.

Be the King or Queen of showing respect and compassion to others. These traits are not popular globally. This doesn't mean that if someone abuses or walks all over you that you take it lying down. Pick your battles and use assertiveness over aggressiveness when slighted. The general demeanor to strive for on a regular basis as much as possible is respect and compassion. Being a compassionate loving person is what garners real attention and attraction from others. If that turns someone off, then don't allow them into your auric circle.

All human beings have both a light and dark ego. The light ego is connected to traits such as having confidence in your abilities, while the dark ego is bogged down in gossip, anger, judgment, or violence. Some dark egos are power addicts. They are much worse than others where a result is desired for individual egotistical advantage. The result can be damaging even if the effect is not in the form of monetary gain. You can still receive a high soaring feeling of emotional satisfaction. Those who are typically giving by nature are not being altruistic for personal pleasure, but for spiritual nourishment. There are various levels of attainment when it comes to altruism.

To be completely selfless is a Divine act possible to achieve. You are made in the likeness of His being. Therefore, you have the capacity of great love and immense selflessness built within you.

Transforming your soul includes evolving in order to see the broader picture. This helps in stripping away the ego, which causes the majority of the sabotage. When you view things from the perception of an egoless being, then you receive that clarity.

There are numerous soul lights threaded around the world doing what they can to offer reminders of the soul's path and to help other souls evolve. This may come in the form of correcting disrespectful behavior, teaching compassionate common-sense etiquette, helping someone through suffering, teaching positive spiritual concepts, helping others have a more peaceful and content life, giving and displaying love, shining at your brightest, and to allowing those in the vicinity to soak that up.

Only love matters, and if parents and teachers around the world all banded together to do their job of teaching love from early on, then that would bring more love like behavior to the planet. While every bit helps, every soul on this gigantic rock needs to partake in it, or the collective consciousness will be no closer to peace and love on Earth than they had ever been.

When you exit this Earthly plane, you leave all of your belongings behind from your job, clothes, money, and all other material possessions. What you recall and take with you on your journey home are the lessons, growth, and connections you made. Whether you are a believer of a higher power, an afterlife or not, why would you waste time not finding a space where love exists? There is nothing joyful about hanging out in an area that has zero love, yet the space that others fall prone to is one of negativity.

Life can be a struggle as you forge on, head down, eyes forward, moving with determination to survive. Your soul desires the kind of rejoicing release that love offers. When you're operating from a high vibration state, then you can come pretty close to that all encompassing all giving love that is fired off from the source naturally. Human souls rely on one another to prop each other up and give a little of bit of that love essence that exists when you reach that high state, but that puts too much pressure on connections that cannot withstand the kind of love that is required as fuel to carry on. You have to stretch higher than that in order to touch the tail end of it. The Earth's dense atmosphere compresses this love due to the domination of the darkness of the ego. It's only when you've re-entered the gates of home does your soul explode by the infusion of this love that permanently baptizes you in its light.

It is the ultimate hope that if you take anything away from this entire piece that you take away love. Love is a simple word that has the power to defeat and kill the Darkness. Whenever you feel like you're struggling or full of stress, anger, or sadness that remember that your soul was made from love. Before you incarnated into the temporary human body you are currently renting, understand that you were made from this love with a purpose. His purpose for you was to carry this love with you while you travel along your soul's many journeys on into infinity and beyond. It is the ammunition you were given to succeed.

As you move about any lifetime in any dimension, you are gaining wisdom through the challenges and experiences you endure wherever you are. This is whether that is through your work endeavors to the various kinds of relationship connections you have from friendships, love, colleagues, acquaintances and family members. When you pass on from this life it is the lessons, knowledge and the love you take with you. It is hoped that as you are crossing over that you understand that Earthly life was the gift in intended to help you remember what love truly is. It is taking the higher angelic view of the superficiality and Darkness that plagues the planet while avoiding getting caught in its web like trap. When you defy the Darkness, then it erupts in anger to see he's lost one of God's warriors to the Light. Become a warrior of love and shine that wherever you roam. When someone agitates you, then re-center and re-align your soul by imagining this love growing bright within you to know that none of that matters. The only thing that ultimately wins in the end is love. Love often, love freely, love bravely and always return to love when you've lost your way.

Acknowledgments

Thank you to God, my Spirit Team Council, and to all of the loyal readers that have hopped on this awesome train ride of mine and stayed on. I am forever blessed and grateful for your eternal support of the work we do. Thank you also for supporting the arts and the artists of the world.

ALSO BY KEVIN HUNTER

Stay Centered Psychic Warrior
Warrior of Light
Empowering Spirit Wisdom
Darkness of Ego
Realm of the Wise One
Transcending Utopia
Reaching for the Warrior Within
Spirit Guides and Angels
Soul Mates and Twin Flames
Raising Your Vibration
Divine Messages for Humanity
Connecting with the Archangels
Monsters and Angels
The Seven Deadly Sins
Love Party of One
Twin Flame Soul Connections
A Beginner's Guide to the Four Psychic Clair Senses
Tarot Card Meanings
Attracting in Abundance
Abundance Enlightenment
Living for the Weekend
Ignite Your Inner Life Force
Awaken Your Creative Spirit
The Essential Kevin Hunter Collection
Metaphysical Divine Wisdom (Series)

STAY CENTERED PSYCHIC WARRIOR

A Psychic Medium's Trip Through the Darkness and Light of the Spirit Worlds, and Other Paranormal Phenomena

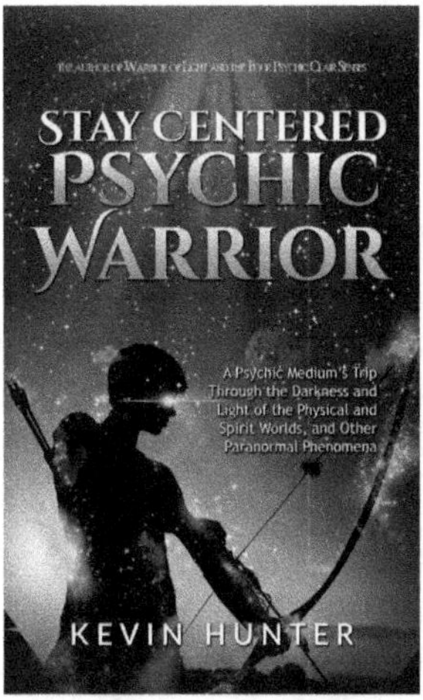

In *Stay Centered Psychic Warrior*, metaphysical teacher, psychic, medium, and author, Kevin Hunter talks about what it's like battling between mental health issues and the deeply potent psychic input that continuously falls into his soul's consciousness throughout each day. He offers plenty of examples and discussions of his brushes with spirit, seeing and hearing the dead, the power of the Darkness and the Light in both the physical and spirit worlds, along with sharing his numerous personal psychic and mediumship essays, glimpses of the Other Side, near death experiences, past lives, soul contracts, traveling to and from the Spirit Worlds, spirit guides and angels, recognizing your own psychic gifts, and much more!

This unique autobiography focuses on psychic and mediumship related content coupled with the soul's journey and purpose. Stay Centered Psychic Warrior is an intensely forceful and revealing read that doesn't shy away from the uncomfortable, the Darkness, abuse, mental health issues, while uplifting it with the many blessings of the Light and intriguing day to day psychic phenomena all in one. Allow it to inspire you to recognize your own psychic gifts knowing there is much more to this Earthly life than can be seen or comprehended. Be empowered to break through the rubble and stand strong and centered under the powerful Light that shines through any Darkness.

A Beginner's Guide to the FOUR PSYCHIC CLAIR SENSES

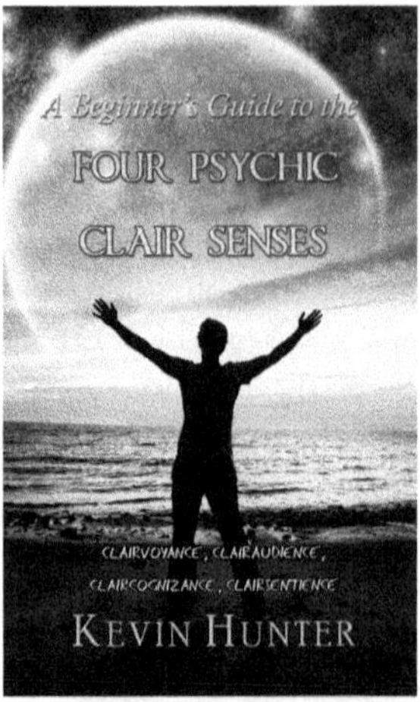

Many believe psychic gifts are bestowed upon select chosen ones, while others don't believe in the craft at all. The reality is every soul is born with heightened psychic gifts and capabilities, but somewhere along the way those senses have dimmed. All are capable of being a conduit with the Other Side, including those closed off and blocked to it. There are a variety of enlightened beings residing in the spirit realms to assist human souls that request their help. They use varying means and methods to communicate with you called clair channels. These clairs are crystal clear etheric senses used to communicate with any higher being, spirit guide, angel, departed loved one, archangel, and God.

The *Four Psychic Clair Senses* illustrates what the core senses are, examples of how the author picks up on messages, how you can recognize the guidance, and other fun metaphysical psychic stuff. You are a walking divination tool that allows you to communicate with Spirit. The clairs enable you to receive heavenly messages, guidance, and information that positively assist you or another along your Earthly journey. Read about the four core clairs in order to pinpoint what best describes you and how to have a better understanding of what they are and how they work for you.

TAROT CARD MEANINGS

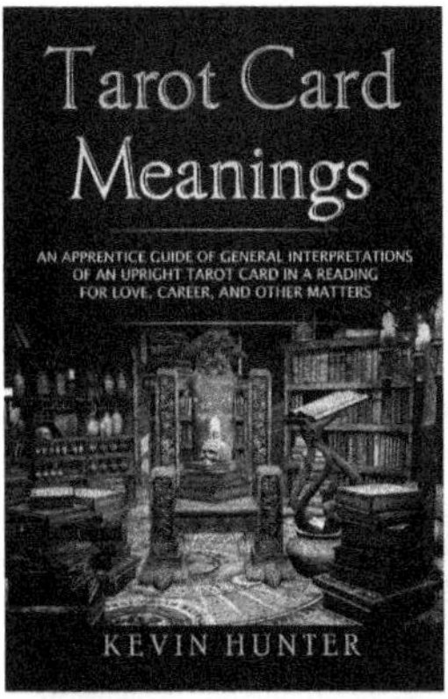

Tarot Card Meanings is an encyclopedia reference guide that takes the Tarot apprentice reader through each of the 78 Tarot Cards offering the potential general meanings and interpretations that could be applied when conducting a reading. The meanings included can be applied to most anything whether it be spiritual, love, general, or work-related questions.

Many novices struggle with reading the Tarot, as they want to know what a card can mean in their readings. They grow stuck staring at three cards side by side and having no idea what it could be telling them. The Tarot Card Meanings book can assist by pointing you in the general direction of where to look. It will not give you the ultimate answers and should not be taken verbatim, as that is up to you as the reader to come to that conclusion. The more you practice, read, and study the Tarot, then the better you become.

Tarot Card Meanings avoids diving into the Tarot history, or card spreads and symbolism, but instead focuses solely on the potential meaning of a card in a general, love, or work reading. This gives you a structure to jump off of, but it is up to you to take that energy and add the additional layers to your reading, while trusting your higher self, intuition, instincts and Spirit team's guidance and messages. Anything included in the Tarot Card Meanings book is an overview and not intended to be gospel. It is merely one suggested version of the potential meanings of each of the 78 Tarot cards in a reading. It may assist the novice that is having trouble interpreting cards for themselves.

ALSO AVAILABLE BY KEVIN HUNTER

Books that Empower, Enlighten, Educate, and Entertain!

Just as your body needs physical food to survive,
your soul needs spiritual food for well-being nourishment.

THE ESSENTIAL KEVIN HUNTER COLLECTION

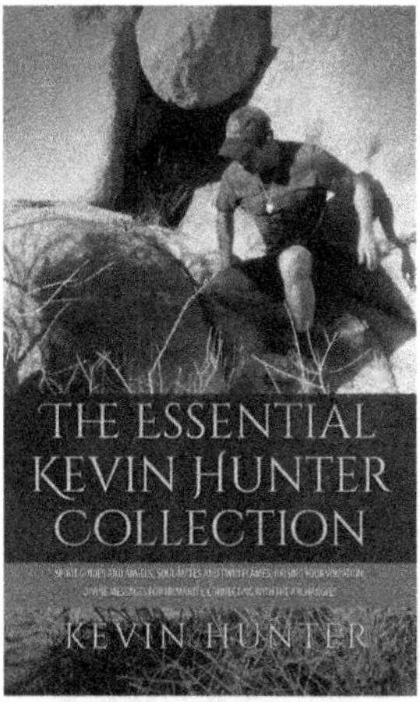

Kevin Hunter an empowering author specializing in a variety of genres, but he is most notably known for his work in the realms of spirituality, metaphysical, and self-help. He has assisted people around the world with standing in their power, and in having a stronger connection with Heaven, while navigating the materialistic practical world. Now some of his popular spiritually based books are available in this one gigantic volume.

The Essential Kevin Hunter Collection is the spiritual bible that contains over 500 pages of content geared towards improving and enhancing your life. It is for those who prefer to have everything in one gigantic book. The content included in this edition are from the books: *Spirit Guides and Angels, Soul Mates and Twin Flames, Raising Your Vibration, Divine Messages for Humanity, Connecting with the Archangels, Warrior of Light, Empowering Spirit Wisdom, and Darkness of Ego.*

TRANSCENDING UTOPIA

Reopening the Pathway to Divinity

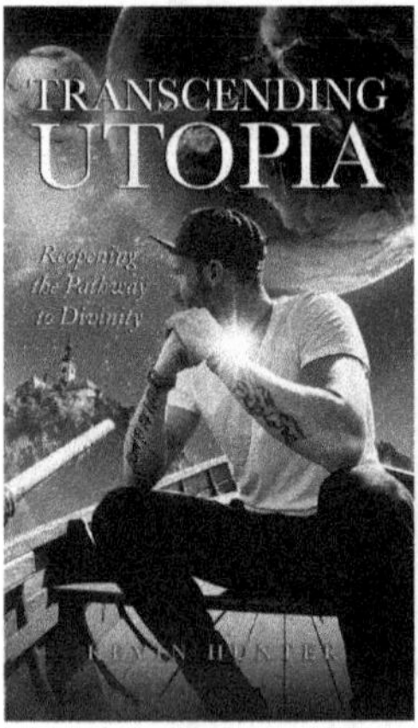

Transcending Utopia is packed with practical and spirit knowledge that focuses on enhancing your life through empowering divinely guided spiritual related teachings, inspiration, wisdom, guidance, and messages. The way to accelerate existence on Earth towards Utopia is if every person on the planet resided in their soul's true nature, which is in a state of all love, joy, and peace. The ultimate Nirvana is surpassing that perfection through methods that a limited consciousness could ever dream possible. This is the exceptional glory your soul was born into before the dense turbulence of Earthly life enveloped and suffocated you.

Transcending Utopia is to go beyond your limits and travel outside of the generic mundane materialistic achievement that human beings taught one another to thrive for. A utopian society is where everything is perfectly blissful on all levels according to the sanctified values you were born with. The sensations connected to how flawless everything feels in that moment reveals the authentic perfection you were made from. Utopia is the ideal paradise as imagined in one's dreams that seems to be inaccessible by human standards. It is a state of mind that is possible to reach by adopting broader ways of looking at circumstances while being disciplined about how you conduct your life. You search for a sign of this utopia through external means, only to be consistently left with disappointment. This is because utopia begins and ends inside the spark that burns within your spirit like a pilot light waiting to be ignited.

LIVING FOR THE WEEKEND

The Winding Road Towards Balancing Career Work and Spiritual Life

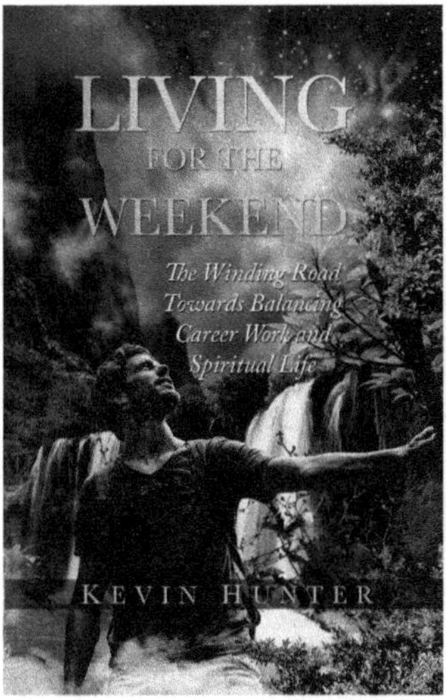

Working hard to ensure your bills are paid can leave your soul spiritually starved for soul nourishment. When your ultimate goal is to obtain enough money to be comfortable that you become carried away in that current, then there is little to no room for Divine enrichment.

Many work to survive in jobs they hate because it's the way it is. As a result, they experience and endure all sorts of emotional pain whether it is through depression, sadness, anger, or any other kind of negative stressor. Some silently suffer through this emotional strain gradually killing off their life force. If you don't have a healthy social life and positive fun filled activities and hobbies to balance that burden outside of that, then that could add additional tension. What's it all for if you can't live the life you've always wanted to live? Instead, you spend your days growing forever miserable and broken.

Living for the Weekend examines the pitfalls, struggles, as well as the benefits available in the current modern-day working world. This is followed up with spiritual and practical tips, guidance, messages, and discussions on ways to incorporate more balance and enlightenment to a cutthroat material driven world.

Attracting in Abundance

Opening the Divine Gates to Inviting in Blessings and Prosperity Through Body, Mind, and Soul Spirit

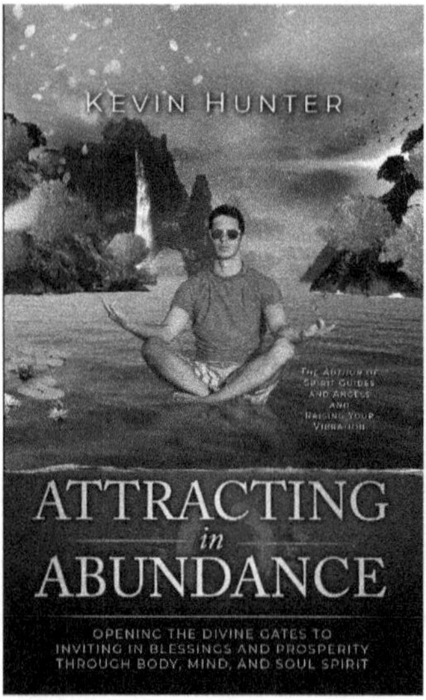

Having enough money to survive comfortably enough on this physical plane is part of obtaining abundance, but it's not the destination and purpose to thrive for. You could work hard to make enough money to the point you are set for life, but that won't necessarily equate to happiness. Achieving a content satisfied state of joy and serenity starts with examining your soul's state and overall well-being. When that's in place, then the rest will follow.

Attracting in Abundance combines practical and spirit wisdom surrounding the nature of abundance. This is something that most everyone can get on board with because all human beings desire physical comforts, blessings, and prosperity, regardless of their personal values and belief systems. *Attracting in Abundance* is broken up into three parts to help move you towards inviting abundance into your life on all levels. "Part One" contains some no-nonsense lectures surrounding the philosophies, concepts, and debates on the laws of attracting in abundance. "Part Two" is the largest of the sections geared towards fine tuning the soul into preparing for abundance. "Part Three" is the final lesson plan to help crack open the gates of abundance with various helpful tidbits, guidance, and messages as well as the blocks that can prevent abundance from coming in.

The B-Side to the Attracting in Abundance book

ABUNDANCE ENLIGHTENMENT

*An Easy Motivational Guide to
the Laws of Attracting in Abundance
and Transforming Your Soul*

Ultimate authentic success surrounds your soul's growth and evolving process. It's when you realize that none of the physical ego driven desires matter in the end. You can work hard to make sure you stay afloat, you're able to pay your bills, and support yourself and family, but you're not chasing popularity for external validation. Any amount of goodness displayed from your heart is the true measure of real accomplishment.

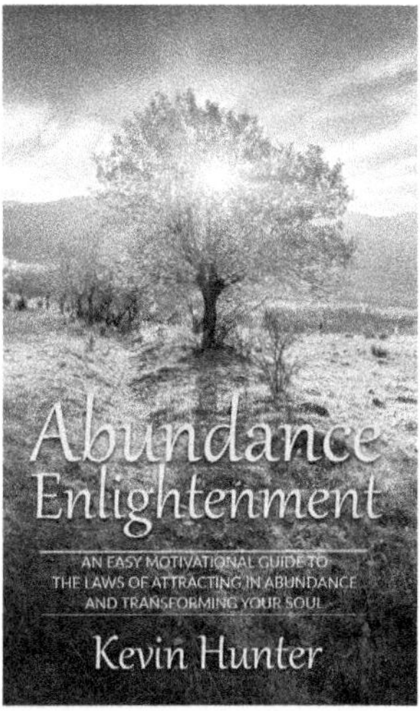

An overflowing feeling of optimism and love coupled with faith and action is what increases the chances of attracting good things and positive experiences to you. Abundance is more than monetary and financial increase. It can also be about reaching an optimistic well-being state of joy, peace, and love. This positive emotional mindful state simultaneously attracts in blessings.

Abundance Enlightenment is the follow up book to *Attracting in Abundance*. It contains both practical guidance and spirit wisdom that can be applied to everyday life. Some of the key topics surround the laws of attraction as well as healthier money management and improving your soul to help make you a fine tuned in abundance attractor.

MONSTERS AND ANGELS

An Empath's Guide to Finding Peace in a Technologically Driven World Ripe with Toxic Monsters and Energy Draining Vampires

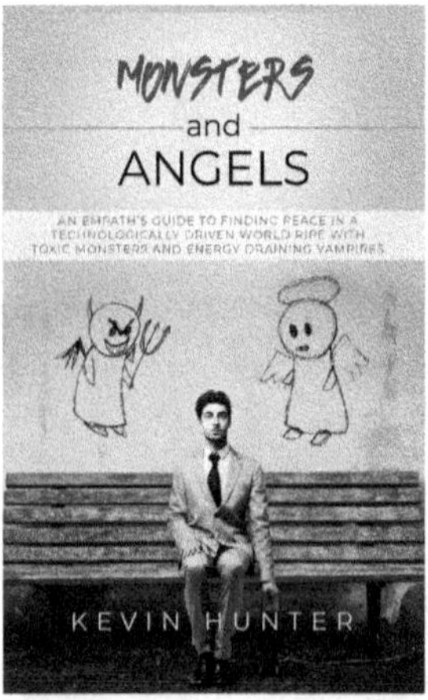

Every person on the planet is capable of being empathic and sensitive, to becoming an energy vampire or toxic monster. No one is exempt from displaying the darker sides of their ego. The easiest and most efficient way to spread any kind of energy is online. Every time you log onto the Internet, there is a larger chance you're going to see something related to the news, media, or gossip areas thrown in front of you, even if you attempt to avoid it as much as possible. You're absorbing everything that your consciousness faces, including the ugly and the wicked, which has its own consequences. This tempestuous energy is tossed into the Universe ultimately creating a flame-throwing battleground inside and around you.

Monsters and Angels discusses how technology, media, and social media have an immense power in distributing both positive and negative influences far and wide. This is about being mindful of what can negatively affect your state of being, and how to counter and avoid that when and wherever possible. This is why it's beneficial to govern yourself, your life, and your surroundings like a strict disciplined executive.

TWIN FLAME SOUL CONNECTIONS

Recognizing the Split Apart, the Truths and Myths of Twin Flames, Soul Love Connections, Soul Mates, and Karmic Relationships

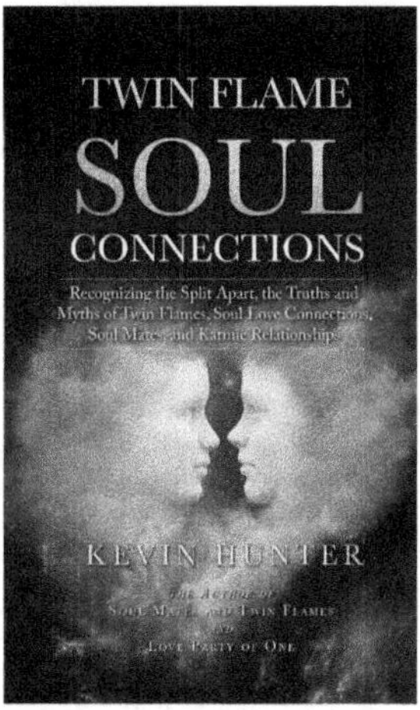

Twin Flames have a shared ongoing sentiment and quest from the moment they're a spark shooting out of God's love that explodes into a blinding white fire that breaks apart causing one to be two, until two become one again, separate and whole, and back around again. Looking into the eyes of your Twin Flame is like looking into the eyes of God, because to know love is to know God.

Twin Flame Soul Connections discusses and lists some of the various myths and truths surrounding the Twin Flames, and how to identify if you've come into contact with your Twin Flame, or if you know someone who has. The ultimate goal is not to find ones Twin Flame, but to awaken one's heart to love, and to work on becoming complete and whole as an individual soul through spiritual self-mastery, life lessons, growth, and raising your consciousness. Your soul's life was born out of love and will die right back into that love.

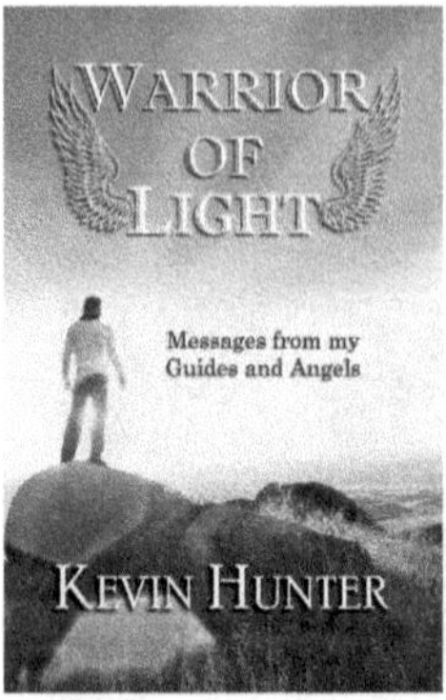

WARRIOR OF LIGHT

Messages from my Guides and Angels

There are legions of angels, spirit guides, and departed loved ones in heaven that watch and guide you on your journey here on Earth. They are around to make your life easier and less stressful. Learn how you can recognize the guidance of your own Spirit team of guides and angels around you. Author, Kevin Hunter, relays heavenly guided messages about getting humanity, the world, and yourself into shape. He delivers the guidance passed onto him by his own Spirit team on how to fine tune your body, soul and raise your vibration. Doing this can help you gain hope and faith in your own life in order to start attracting in more abundance.

EMPOWERING SPIRIT WISDOM

A Warrior of Light's Guide on Love, Career and the Spirit World

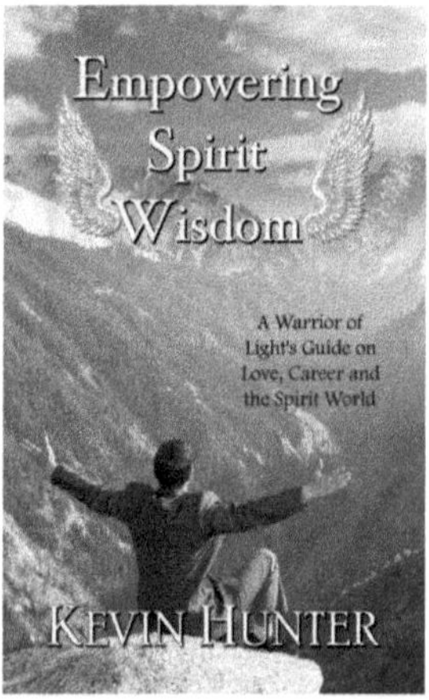

Kevin Hunter relays heavenly, guided messages for everyday life concerns with his book, *Empowering Spirit Wisdom.* Some of the topics covered are your soul, spirit and the power of the light, laws of attraction, finding meaningful work, transforming your professional and personal life, navigating through the various stages of dating and love relationships, as well as other practical affirmations and messages from the Archangels. Kevin Hunter passes on the sensible wisdom given to him by his own Spirit team in this inspirational book.

DARKNESS OF EGO

In *Darkness of Ego*, author Kevin Hunter infuses some of the guidance, messages, and wisdom he's received from his Spirit team surrounding all things ego related. The ego is one of the most damaging culprits in human life. Therefore, it is essential to understand the nature of the beast in order to navigate gracefully out of it when it spins out of control. Some of the topics covered in *Darkness of Ego* are humanity's destruction, mass hysteria, karmic debt, and the power of the mind, heaven's gate, the ego's war on love and relationships, and much more.

REACHING FOR THE WARRIOR WITHIN

Reaching for the Warrior Within is the author's personal story recounting a volatile childhood. This led him to a path of addictions, anxiety and overindulgence in alcohol, drugs, cigarettes and destructive relationships. As a survival mechanism, he split into many different "selves". He credits turning his life around, not by therapy, but by simultaneously paying attention to the messages he has been receiving from his Spirit team in Heaven since birth.

REALM OF THE WISE ONE

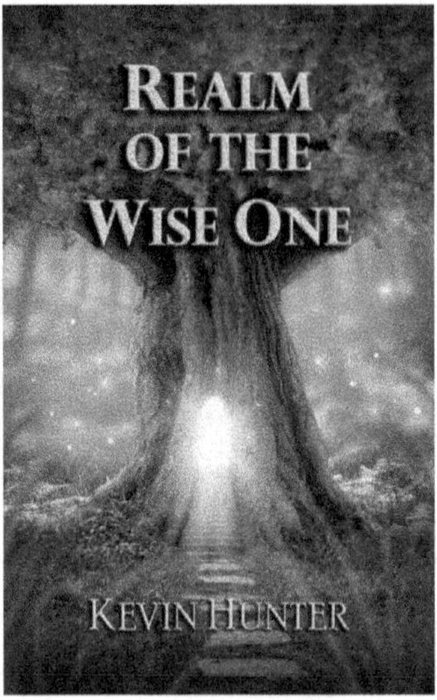

In the Spirit Worlds and the dimensions that exist, reside numerous kingdoms that house a plethora of Spirits that inhabit various forms. One of these tribes is called the Wise Ones, a darker breed in the spirit realm who often chooses to incarnate into a human body one lifetime after another for important purposes.

The *Realm of the Wise One* takes you on a magical journey to the spirit world where the Wise Ones dwell. This is followed with in-depth and detailed information on how to recognize a human soul who has incarnated from the Wise One Realm. Author, Kevin Hunter, is a Wise One who uses the knowledge passed onto him by his Spirit team of Guides and Angels to relay the wisdom surrounding all things Wise One. He discusses the traits, purposes, gifts, roles, and personalities among other things that make up someone who is a Wise One. Wise Ones have come in the guises of teachers, shaman, leaders, hunters, mediums, entertainers and others. *Realm of the Wise One* is an informational guide devoted to the tribe of the Wise Ones, both in human form and on the Other Side.

IGNITE YOUR INNER LIFE FORCE

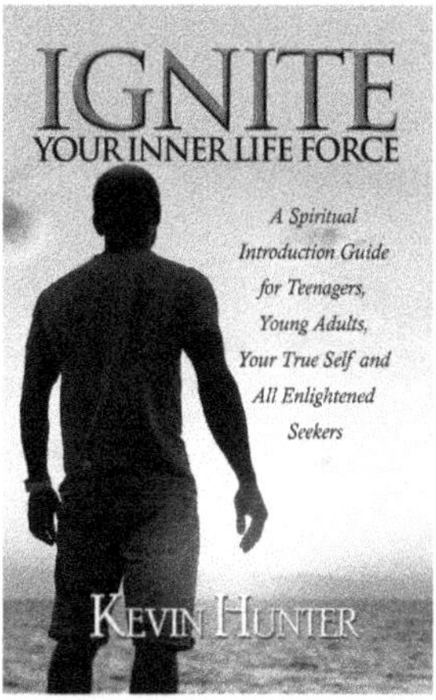

Ignite Your Inner Life Force is an introduction guide for teens, young adults, and anyone seeking answers, messages, and guidance and surrounding spiritual empowerment. This is from understanding what Heaven, the soul, and spiritual beings are to knowing when you are connecting with your Spirit team of Guides and Angels. Some of the topics covered are communicating with Heaven, working with your Spirit team, what your higher self is, your life purpose and soul contract, what the ego is, love and relationships, your vibration energy, shifting your consciousness and thinking for yourself even when you stand alone. This is an in-depth primer manual offering you foundation as you find a higher purpose navigating through your personal journey in today's modern-day practical world.

AWAKEN YOUR CREATIVE SPIRIT

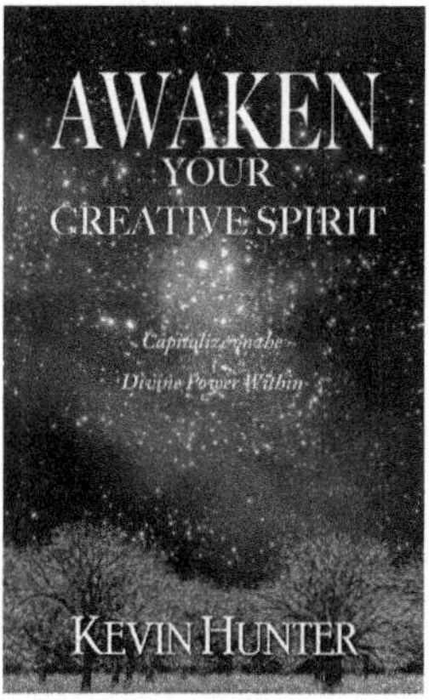

Your creative spirit is more than being artistic and getting involved in creativity pursuits, although this is a good part of it. When your creative spirit is activated by a high vibration state of being, then this is the space you create from. You can apply this to your dealings in life, your creative and artistic pursuits, and to having a greater communication line with your Spirit team on the Other Side. *Awaken Your Creative Spirit* is an overview of what it means to have access to Divine assistance and how that plays a part in arousing the muse within you in order to bring your state of mind into a happier space.

THE *WARRIOR OF LIGHT* SERIES OF POCKET BOOKS

Spirit Guides and Angels, Soul Mates and Twin Flames, Raising Your Vibration, Connecting with the Archangels, Twin Flame Soul Connections, Attracting in Abundance, Monsters and Angels, The Four Psychic Clair Senses, The Seven Deadly Sins, Love Party of One, Abundance Enlightenment, and *Divine Messages for Humanity*

METAPHYSICAL DIVINE WISDOM
BOOK SERIES

On Psychic Spirit Team Heaven Communication
On Soul Consciousness and Purpose
On Increasing Prayer with Faith for an Abundant Life
On Balancing the Mind, Body, and Soul
On Manifesting Fearless Assertive Confidence
On Universal, Physical, Spiritual and Soul Love

♥

About Kevin Hunter

Kevin Hunter is the metaphysical author of dozens of spiritually based books that include *Warrior of Light, Transcending Utopia, Stay Centered Psychic Warrior, Metaphysical Divine Wisdom Series, Empowering Spirit Wisdom, Realm of the Wise One, Reaching for the Warrior Within, Darkness of Ego, Living for the Weekend, Ignite Your Inner Life Force, Awaken Your Creative Spirit,* and *Tarot Card Meanings.*

His pocket books include, *Spirit Guides and Angels, Soul Mates and Twin Flames, Raising Your Vibration, Divine Messages for Humanity, Connecting with the Archangels, The Seven Deadly Sins, Four Psychic Clair Senses, Monsters and Angels, Twin Flame Soul Connections, Attracting in Abundance, Love Party of One* and *Abundance Enlightenment.* His non-spiritual related works include the horror drama, *Paint the Silence,* and the modern-day love story, *Jagger's Revolution.*

Kevin started out in the entertainment business in 1996 as the personal development assistant guy to one of Hollywood's most respected acting talents, Michelle Pfeiffer, at her former boutique production company, Via Rosa Productions. She dissolved her company after several years and he made a move into coordinating film productions for the studios. His film credits include One Fine Day, A Thousand Acres, The Deep End of the Ocean, Crazy in Alabama, The Perfect Storm, Original Sin, Harry Potter & the Sorcerer's Stone, Dr. Dolittle 2, and Carolina. He considers himself a beach bum born and raised in Southern California. For more information and books visit: www.kevin-hunter.com

www.ingramcontent.com/pod-product-compliance
Lightning Source LLC
Chambersburg PA
CBHW070104070426
42448CB00038B/1431
* 9 7 8 1 7 3 3 1 9 6 2 5 3 *